Gallipoli 1915

Titles in the 'Fortunes of War' series

FORTUNES OF WAR

Gallipoli 1915

JOSEPH MURRAY

CERBERUS

First published by William Kimber and Co Ltd in 1965

PUBLISHED IN THE UNITED KINGDOM BY;
Cerberus Publishing Limited
22A Osprey Court
Hawkfield Business Park
Bristol
BS14 0BB
UK
e-mail: cerberusbooks@aol.com
www.cerberus-publishing.com

British Library Cataloguing in Publication Data
A catalogue record for this book is available from the British Library.

940.
426

ISBN 1 84145 047 2   1483873

PRINTED AND BOUND IN ENGLAND.

Contents

INTRODUCTION

Joseph Murray was the son of a Scots miner who lived and worked in County Durham. The boy was educated at the Leazes Council School, Burnopfield, but left at the age of twelve to work in the mines himself. It had to be proved to the authorities that it was essential that he should do so to provide additional money for the home.

During the Gallipoli campaign, Murray, who had the remarkable experience of going through the whole fighting from the landing to the evacuation without a serious wound, kept a rough diary on scraps of paper, some of which he sent home and others he kept with him. Later in Spitzbergen, when engaged in mining exploration, he pieced the scraps together and made a rough narrative, and later he wrote the present book from this material. The general historical background to the events in which he was a participant may be summarised as follows:

At the beginning of the 1914 war, Turkey's position was that of an unstable neutral. The Young Turks were in power, a revolutionary party not entirely acceptable to the British Government. The German Military Mission under Liman von Sanders dominated the Turkish Army; the British Military Mission had rather less control of the Turkish Navy. Then, towards the end of September 1914, a German officer authorised the closing of the Dardanelles by mines, a flagrant breach of Turkish neutrality, and a month later Turkey was at war on the German side. The importance to Britain was this: the Black Sea was now effectively sealed off from the Mediterranean and the vital supply line to her Russian ally was cut.

By April 1915 the war in France and Flanders had reached a trench-bound stalemate. The vast Russian armies had suffered defeat at Tannenberg and the Masurian Lakes; they wanted help in the form of arms and ammunition; and they wanted the Turks distracted from their campaigns in the Caucasus. If Russia collapsed, Germany's most serious worry, that of fighting a war on two fronts, was gone. The situation revived an old idea of Winston Churchill, the First Lord of the Admiralty, an operation to force the Dardanelles and seize Constantinople. Kitchener made it clear that he could spare no troops from the main battlefields, and so the first plans were for a primarily naval assault.

In March 1915 a combined Franco-British force attempted to sail up the Dardanelles; as they reached the Narrows and victory seemed in sight, three battleships fell victims to mines, and the operation was temporarily halted and finally given up. It was now clear that the Navy could not do the whole job themselves. A combined operation was planned and launched on 25th April, 1915. The command of the Army was given to General Ian Hamilton, who was told by Kitchener; 'If the Fleet gets through, Constantinople will fall of itself and you will have won not a battle, but the war.'

In the weeks following the naval attack, the Turks had not been idle. The command of the force defending the Dardanelles was given to Liman von Sanders; he had six divisions, and he disposed them with extraordinary skill. The Allied Force consisted of 75,000 men: the Anzac Corps – two divisions, one Australian and one New Zealand; 29th British Division; a French division; and the Royal Naval Division, to which Joseph Murray belonged. The Anzacs landed at Gaba Tepe; 29th Division at Cape Helles, to be joined by the French, who had made an unsuccessful attempt to establish a bridgehead at Kum Kale, and the Royal Naval Division, which had first staged a diversionary mock-landing further up the peninsula, to keep the Turkish troops widely dispersed. The Cape Helles landing was reasonably successful, but Mount Achi Baba, which dominated the whole bridgehead, was not captured in the first few days as planned, and indeed never was. The Anzacs only established themselves on a narrow strip of cliffside which was overlooked at close quarters by the Turkish positions. Attempts to break out of the two separated bridgeheads were unsuccessful and incurred heavy loss of life.

The situation was again a stalemate, but the casualties continued to mount It was decided that the only way out of the deadlock was a fresh landing, to be made at Suvla Bay, further to the north. General Hamilton now had 120,000 men available in all; the Turks numbered about the same. On 6th August a force of 20,000 men was landed at Suvla Bay; in spite of their taking the Turks partially by surprise, and tremendous support from the Anzacs, at the end of twenty-four hours they had barely advanced two miles. It was not enough, The battle dragged on for a further three weeks but achieved practically nothing.

In October, the first plans for evacuation were discussed; by December, rumours had spread round the fighting men. The Anzac and Suvla Bay positions were abandoned on the 19th December. The four divisions at Cape Helles held on alone against twenty-one Turkish divisions. On 8th January 1916 the last British troops were safely evacuated from Cape Helles. The Gallipoli campaign was over.

CHAPTER ONE

PREPARATION

I had heard old soldiers speak of war as one glorious adventure, full of heroic episodes that could be related to their enthralled listeners without fear of contradiction; tales of far off countries so vastly different to this merry old England.

We who stayed at home or were not old enough to have ventured upon the glorious peregrinations felt miserable and longed to grow up, to grow old enough to pack up and join these voyages of adventure.

Old soldiers Joe Cameron, Jos Brannon, Kit Oloy and Josie Hinaghan had just come back from South Africa and I can well remember as a boy the great welcome accorded to them in my own home village. Effigies of Kruger hung across the street and the mass of flames from the bonfires seemed to me to be about to set the whole village on fire. The heroes had returned victorious from the war and all was merry and bright. Each and every day since then they had related their wonderful experiences with just pride; they had had such a glorious time chasing the raggy old Boers and they spoke of having had their pockets filled with diamonds – real diamonds!

Why was I not old enough? Why was I debarred from taking part in this wonderful war? Then I would have been amongst the heroes and everyone would have been wanting to talk with me. I would have had plenty of money – not really needed, as everything for the heroes was free. They had nothing to do but to stroll in uniform down to Burnopfield or over to West Stanley, shaking hands with almost everyone they met They, could not possibly have known all these people – it must have been the uniform. Everyone must have known that they were fresh from the war; their sun-tan was such a contrast to the pale faces of the miners who saw precious little of the sun.

At each anniversary of the Relief of Mafeking the heroes, with medals adorning their breasts and led by the local band, attended church parades. Childlike I would join the marchers, only to find it most difficult to keep in step. When I corrected my step I was several yards behind and had to run to resume my place in the procession, only to find myself out of step again. At the church, only the adults were allowed inside but when the service was over we youngsters again joined the procession back to the village.

In the evening each ballast-heap in the district had its own bonfire and fireworks display. There must have been huge parades in London and the big cities and thousands of people were celebrating. I felt that I must go to London ope day and see for myself and maybe join in.

Thus passed each anniversary until the new war came and the old war – and its heroes – were forgotten.

One day Mother was very angry and threw my eldest brother's collar on to the fire. Tom said he was going out and soon got another collar, but Mother put that on the fire also and said she would thrash him if he went out. In fact, she said, he ought to go to bed – and I should have been there long ago. I wanted some supper but was afraid to ask, so I hurried up-stairs to avoid the row that seemed inevitable.

When I arose early the next morning. Mother appeared to have been crying all night. Father had not gone to work, nor had Tom, and their working clothes were still hanging up. Tom must have gone out late last night after all and Father also to look for him.

Why all this fuss? Why was Mother crying and why should Tom go out so late at night? Where had he gone? He should have been at work and so should Father.

I went off to school and on returning home as usual at about four-thirty I found Mother still crying. She must have been crying all day as well as all night. Neither Father nor Tom had returned and I hurried along to the Co-op at Burnopfleld with the order for our food. It should have been ready for the order-man when he called that morning. My brother Willie was having his tea; we always called it tea but it was dinner really.

It was dark when I got home although I ran most of the way. Mother had told me to hurry, so I did.

Father was home again. He had got to know from someone that Tom had joined the Royal Navy. But why should he look so miserable and worried? Why should Mother still cry? Tom had only joined the Navy and would sail round the world in a big battleship. Would washing the deck in his bare feet give him nasty colds? Was that what was making Mother cry?

The next day Tom wrote and said be was at Portsmouth, having passed through London on his way. He said he thought he would like the life and everybody was very friendly. He was sorry he had upset Mother but he wanted to travel abroad and the only chance he had of doing this was by joining the Navy. He had thought it over for a long time. He had signed on for five years and seven years on the Reserve. There was nothing to worry about and he would write often.

As time passed we had letters and picture post-cards from Africa, India, Rio, Valparaiso, China, Japan, Australia, Samoa, America, Canada and Vladivostok; pictures of the Suez Canal, Constantinople, Gibraltar, Naples and of the great earthquake at Messina where almost every building was destroyed yet several crucifixes stood defiant amongst the ruins.

Tom had seen the world and when he came home on leave it.was a great pleasure for me to sit and listen to him describing the wonderful things he had seen. When he left to rejoin his ship, the Good Hope, at least fifty people went to the station to see him off, singing and dancing on the way. Everyone was in good spirits with an extra bottle on hand, except Mother. It was always a sad day for poor old Mother when he had to leave. Even when be had finished his service and had to go for a month's training with the Special Reserve she was upset. He used to tell her it was his month's holiday. There was always the usual crowd and they did their best also to convince her but, I'm afraid, to no avail.

One fine day in June 1914, Tom left for his training but, at his special request, he went alone to the station. It seemed very strange. I can see him now walking across the cricket field towards the railway line that was used to transport the coal. from the Lintz Colliery to the North Eastern Railway siding at Friarside. This was a short cut to the station and he was soon out of sight.

As time went on, we heard that he had rejoined his old ship, HMS *Good Hope*. He and all those at home were delighted. He had been in this ship when Sir Percy Scott made her his Flagship on his memorable 60,000 miles cruise. Our pleasure, however, was cut short. Tom was due to come, home but the sky had darkened and war clouds had blotted out the July sunshine. I heard a lot of talk of treaties between this country and that country. If Russia did this, then France would do that, and if Austria wanted help, then Germany must go to her aid. It all seemed to be a matter of 'ifs'.

The position was soon clarified. Germany, in order to out-flank the French armies, invaded Belgium. Britain was pledged to aid Belgium and so the whole of Europe was ablaze.

It could not last very long – it was too gigantic – only a matter of a month or so at the most.

Tom had quite recently told me that we would soon be at war with Germany. He advised me to join the Navy or the Territorials because if the Germans did get here, we could then take up arms to defend our home. If we were unlucky enough to be caught, we would be regarded and treated as prisoners of war, but if we had not served in the armed forces and were caught with any kind of firearm, we would be shot on the spot as spies.

Kitchener asked for three million volunteers for three years or for the duration of the war. He, apparently, did not think it would be over before Christmas.

Winston Churchill asked for volunteers for the Royal Naval Volunteer Reserve, to operate as Naval Brigades. I remember Tom telling me of the wonderful contribution of a Naval Brigade to the South African War; how they mounted some smaller naval guns on carriages and took them ashore – handy lads, these Naval chaps.

Having in mind that the war would not last long, I decided to join the Royal Naval Volunteer Reserve and on Tuesday night, October 6th, I walked to Elswick, a distance of eight miles, and joined the queue on board HMS *Calliope* lying in the Tyne. Our names and addresses were taken and we were told to report on board on Saturday, October 18th, for medical examination.

It was very late when I arrived home and everyone had gone to bed. In my very clumsy way I attempted to preserve the silence but I apparently disturbed Mother – maybe she was already awake. She asked me where I had been until this late and, after saying I thought she was asleep, I said I had been to the pictures at West Stanley. Not wishing to tell her any more lies, I bade her 'Goodnight' and rather hurriedly went off to bed. As soon as I got upstairs I wished I had told her the truth. Somehow she seemed to know I had told her lie. Should I go down and tell her the truth? Suppose on Saturday I failed to pass the medical examination? I was not quite sure myself whether I had enlisted or not. I had volunteered but had I been accepted? I decided to let it go until I knew for certain I had been accepted and then I would tell Mother. It would be foolish to worry her for nothing.

I did not sleep well, I was too excited. In the morning I went off to work as usual The conversation was all about war. I did not enter into it but listened to everything that was said. The war was very interesting to me now; maybe I was even part of it.

On Saturday, October 10th, I finished work at twelve o'clock and was anxious to get home and changed. I had to report for my medical that day. Eddie Kelly, a pal of mine, had agreed to come with me and was to meet me at the Institute. I was a little late because mother seemed to know where I was going and to me it appeared that she was deliberately delaying me. But how could she know? – no one knew, not even Eddie Kelly. He did not know I had volunteered on Tuesday and had only agreed to come with me less than an hour before on our way home from work.

It was one-thirty when I finally arrived at the Institute and Eddie and I started our eight mile walk to Elswick. I told him I had already been there last Tuesday but was not sure of the outcome; I would know today.

We were very tired when we arrived on board the *Calliope* as we had been up since three in the morning. However, once aboard, the questioning began all over again. I said I had answered all these questions on Tuesday.

'Well, answer them again;' said the Petty Officer. 'How old are you? What is your full name and address? Your fathers name?'

They even asked me if I knew my religion! What was that to do with fighting? Eddie was told to stand to one side; he had said he was eighteen but he was only sixteen.

'How old do you say you are Sonny?'

'Eighteen, sir.'

'Very well, Sonny. Just bring your birth certificate along with you on Monday and you will be able to go with your pal'

Looking very gloomy, he agreed to wait for me. I was instructed to go down below and undress. The room was crowded and I felt awfully shy but, in case they would not have me, obeyed at once. We had to stand naked in a row so that the medical man could inspect the soles of our feet

'Stand upon your right leg' was the next order and almost the whole line fell over. Some of the chaps had utmost difficulty in standing on both legs, let alone one.

After a little while we were given a thorough examination and then told to dress. After what seemed ages we were told then that we could go home and they would let us know, that is, those who had passed, when they needed us. This cast a gloom over all of us as we thought that, having passed the medical examination, we would go into training at once. At this rate, the war would be over before we were ready.

Eddie and I caught a train home and I was having supper when Father came in. He said his tender for a big job had been accepted and he would require at least another hundred men to carry it out. I think he had had a little celebration before he came home – he was certainly in a merry mood. It was his custom on such occasions to have a party when he would air his knowledge of the plays of Shakespeare by standing on a chair and reciting in a most professional way: 'Lay on, Macbeth, and damned be he' – and so on and on. I had heard these quotations so often I could recite them at win. They usually bored me stiff, but not tonight His jocular mood then changed to one of seriousness. He was a real orator; I had not noticed this quality before. With the eloquence of Mark Antony, he spoke not of Julius Caesar, but of the war. He said it would last and every man-Jack would be needed, and aye, every women too. Before it was over half of Europe would be eating grass.

At that moment I plucked up courage to tell Father that I had joined the RNVR The news astounded him. He remained quiet for a moment and then shook me by the hand for the first time in his life. My childhood had terminated and in a few brief moments I had become a man. I felt very proud indeed. I could read in his face that, although he knew that sooner or later we would all have to go – he had only a few moments ago said so – he was pleased I had shown enough courage to join up before being compelled to do so. He would have preferred that I had enlisted in Mr Shield's battalions. Mr Shield, who was the son of the owner of our mine, was a captain in the Territorials and was forming a battalion. I had given this considerable thought but had decided that if I joined this battalion I would have to wait until the requisite number of men had enlisted and then there would be at least six months training in England, whereas if I joined the RNVR, I would be on the spot immediately. Part of my training would be aboard ship and I would be at sea; I might even see some fighting at once.

At work on Monday, I had occasion to tell several of my workmates that I had enlisted. A certain Joseph Hannen would not believe me and bet me a shilling I would not go.

The week seemed to drag, but on Saturday morning I received a notification to report on board at eight in the evening on Monday, October 19th, for draft to the Crystal Palace.

I was thrilled-I was going to be in time after all. Mother was, obviously worried and I felt sorry for her and kept out of her way. I decided to go to work as usual on Monday as I should be home by four-thirty and would have plenty of time to get to Elswick by eight.

Monday morning, however, found me sleeping peacefully when I should have been at work. When I woke I asked Mother; why she had not called me: She said I would need all my strength for the long journey ahead and she didn't need the money, anyway.

After an excellent meal I went for a long walk alone during which I visualised all manner of things. I thought of the visit to the far off countries that Tom had told me about, but never once thought of war. Passing through my mind was the whole of Tom's sea-going life and in my imagination I was touring the world. I was pleased with myself, pleased that my chance in life had come and I had taken it. My life was about to begin in earnest.

Arriving home well before my father and brothers, I waited for tea-time: Mother took this opportunity to tell me that I was foolish to enlist as there were plenty of older lads that should go first. Tom was already there and one from the family was quite enough.

'Why did you enlist?'

I replied that I simply thought I must. Something had told me I should and, as I wished to see the world, this was my great opportunity.

'Do not worry. Mother. I shall come back safely enough, I am positive of that'

My remarks seemed to have exactly the opposite effect to what I had intended. My intention was to console her, but I had very much upset her and she was sobbing bitterly. Why had I not a classical education so that I could express myself more clearly? With all the goodwill in the world I had endeavoured to console her but had only succeeded in making things worse. I felt awful. What could I say to stop those tears?

'Look here, Mother, try to buck up. I have only a few short hours left with you and here you are making me miserable. Thousands of young lads have gone and thousands more will follow, so why not me? Surely if they can stand up to it, I can. Do you remember when I was working in the pit and young Peter Hanratty backed his restless pony on to those three fun tubs with only me behind to hold them? I could not hold them – I'm not Samson. The gallery was less than a yard high and I ran over fifty yards in the dark with the three tubs chasing after me. What happened? I fell down out of breath and could not get up. I waited for the wagons to smash me to pieces but they didn't. They jumped the rails only a couple of feet away from me and brought the roof down. The stone and timber fell about me in such a way that it had to be cleared before they could get me free. I was not hurt – frightened, that's all. I know they brought me home but that was because I could not stop being sick. I am only a youngster but I believe that we all have an allotted span and when the time comes for us to go, it doesn't matter where we are or what we are doing. If we have run the course, the race is finished.'

Our conversation was interrupted by the arrival of my brothers, Eddie and Robert.

'Hello, Joe, what train are you catching?'

Turning to sister Margaret they asked her to prepare some hot water so that they could bathe quickly as they expected some friends along to see me off. It seemed only a few minutes before both of them were washed and dressed in their Sunday best and all the family were having tea.

The main topic of conversation was my journey to London. The general consensus of opinion was that I would certainly get a few days' leave at Christmas. Everyone except Mother was happy; well, they appeared to be, anyway.

When tea was over, my other sister, Selina, began giving me Instructions. I was sent off to say 'Goodbye' to our old neighbour, Mrs Wardle, a dear old soul, and, of course, I had to see Geordie Darby who for years had been the official musician, at all parties in the village. One 'Goodbye' after another; I must have said 'Goodbye' to everyone in the village before I arrived at Geordie's house. His wife answered the door and, without watting to be told the object of my visit, informed me that Geordie had gone off, without his dinner, to see me to the station. He must have taken a short cut across the fields, otherwise I would have met him on my way to his house.

According to my calculations, time was getting a bit short I had set off to say 'Goodbye' to a couple of people and had finished by seeing almost everyone. I had to step it out to get back home and I was puffing and blowing like a steam engine when I was met by quite a crowd who had come to see me off. Some of them I knew but the majority I didn't. Geordie had his concertina and was rendering '*Caller Herrin*'.

Mother made me have a cup of tea with her and the crowd moved off, leaving us alone. We had only a few minutes but sufficient time for her to convey to me her motherly feelings and a host of instructions;

'Write as soon as you get there and as often possible. If there is anything you want, just write for it and I will send it at once. I will send you Tom's address as soon as we get it.'

I kissed her goodnight and told her not to worry; I would be home on leave for Christmas.

Mrs Ellis, the lady from next door, came in and, feeling much better now that someone was with Mother, I took my leave. Everyone was very kind. They all exhorted me to take care of myself.

A few days ago I had to think twice before I dared to say 'Good Morning' to anyone, expecting to be told to speak when I was spoken to and not before. Tonight, though, everyone wanted to speak with me – it was all so strange.

All around me people were singing – I could even hear singing in the distance from the station. It sounded like another party on a similar mission and this provoked the natural instinct of the north-countryman to make bets, this time as to who the other party was. Wagers were offered and accepted. Some wagered pounds to pennies; others staked their shirts, their boots, cigars, Woodbines and bottles of Bass or Whisky.

In fact, every conceivable thing was offered and accepted. I cannot say if all these bets were paid in full but, if they were, then some of the party must have felt rather cool minus their shirts and boots. I doubt if the local pub ever carried a sufficient stock of Bass and whisky.

Arriving at the station, we found the platform so crowded that our party had the utmost difficulty in getting on it. The other party we had heard singing had arrived a few minutes before us; they were there to see me off, too. When they had found the main party gone, they had decided to take a short cut across the fields and what a mess they were in. A ploughed field in October is not the ideal tramping ground for anyone, let alone young ladies. The mud had claimed some of their shoes and would not give them up. One lassie had lost both shoes and was being carried, which added to the hilarity. Someone made an impromptu speech which ended with the request that all present should shake hands with the conquering hero and the lassies must kiss him for luck. Whilst this was going on the train arrived and had been signalled to start but the driver thought it better to draw attention by giving a long blast on the whistle. He could not move the train as scores of people were still hanging on to the carriages. The guard came along to see what all the commotion was about but the lassies relieved him of his hat and flag. The hand-shaking, back-slapping and kissing went on; I know some of the lassies had several goes in the queue but, be that as it may, it was not until all were satisfied or exhausted or both, that the train and I could escape. Dozens of them wanted to come with me to Elswiek but I would not allow this.

At last the train began to move and I suddenly realised that I was alone. I was beginning to wish I had allowed someone to accompany me as I desired to talk to someone; I felt awfully lonely.

The train pulled in to Scotswood station and to my great relief and joy several people entered my carriage. I immediately felt easier and much less lonely, but although a few moments before I had wished to talk, I did not now make use of my opportunity and sat silent.

I alighted at Elswiek and walked slowly towards HMS *Calliope*. She was ablaze with lights and from the distance it seemed impossible for any more human beings to stow themselves aboard, but I managed somehow to do this and report to the officer on duty. He told me to remain on board and await further instructions.

'Go and have a dance and enjoy yourself.'

'Everyone was dancing to the ship's band, but I had never been to a dance in my life. Down below, men and their lady friends were playing cards, but I had never been allowed to play cards. For years cards had not been allowed in our house as Mother said they were unlucky. She had good reason for this belief as many years ago Uncle Eddie had been killed in the mine the day following a card-game at home. Uncle Jack and Cousin Tom had suffered in exactly the same way. Not very long ago, whilst Mother was away on her usual shopping expedition to Newcastle, my brother Willie and his three pals were having a quiet game of whist She happened to return earlier than usual aad caught them playing. Snatching the cards, she tore them into shreds and struck out with her fists until the room was empty. I was given the job of sweeping up the pieces and putting then on the fire. Next day Willie and his mates were buried under two tons of coal and rock. Fred Lauder was dead when they got him out and Willie spent quite some time in hospital. We respected Mother's wishes after this and I still cannot play cards.

On the forepart of the deck there was a concert going on and I made myself comfortable, inwardly thankful that there was something I could occupy myself with. I could not sing but I could – and did – listen.

I began to realise that I was nobody's child and my eyes, roaming the audience, fell upon a boy of my own age. He seemed to be as lonely as me. He caught me staring at him and obliged with a smile. I returned his greeting and I at once made a move in his directien. In a matter of minutes we were great friends and we sat chatting until it was time for us to assemble. At about 10 pm, the officer on duty called our names and we, after a struggle, managed to get into some sort of formation.

We marched off the ship and down the Scotswood Road, not to the Blaydon Races as the song says but to the Central Station in Newcastle. We went on to a platform crowded with people awaiting our arrival. It was very difficult for my new friend Tubby, and me to keep together among the hundreds that had marched from the ship.

Everyone except Tubby and I had someone to say farewell to; some were laughing and joking, many were crying and others stood earnestly talking. It was a motley crowd of all ages, vast yet reasonably orderly.

The order to board the train was not altogether obeyed. Tubby and I and many others did obey but there were quite a few who apparently had much more to say to their friends and relatives. In such a crowd no one could have the faintest idea who was travelling and who was staying.

As the train pulled out amidst frantic cheering and a sea of waving handkerchiefs, there were still chaps trying to get aboard. Our compartment was,full and for the first hour or so it resembled an Irish Parliament – everyone talking simultaneously and no one listening. It was past midnight before one by one we began to doze and finally to sleep.

I thought of my home and my people. I had seen Mother on lots of similar occasions when Tom had left after short furloughs. I could visualise her now and I wondered it my efforts to console her had been successful. I thought they had and felt satisfied.

Half asleep, I scrambled out of the train at King's Cross at about seven o'clock on a beautiful morning. I was nearly three hundred miles from my home; my travels had really begun. I was very pleased with myself, having arrived at last in the greatest city in the world, London.

'See Naples and die' they say, but to me, a country bumpkin leaving home for the first time, London was everything. I had never seen so many people or so much traffic.

Breakfast was served on one of the platforms. I say 'served' because that was as far as I got. I just could not swallow the cold half-raw meat or the chunks of bread that had a distinct sawdust look and taste. The tea, like the meat, was cold and greasy; I think they must have ladled it out of a cesspool. Some of the chaps, though, appeared to thoroughly enjoy their first meal in the Navy. Before I left home I had made up my mind to eat everything placed in front of me but I felt ill just looking at this. However, my failure to enjoy my first meal of Service food in no way dampened my spirits. Breakfast was a mis-deal, that was all, and dinner would be an improvement. This of course proved to be blind optimism:

'Now get a move on. You cannot stay here all day – there's a war on, don't you know.'

Of course we all knew this but the Petty Officer persisted in reminding us all again and again.

'Fall in in two ranks, facing the track.' We did this. In contrast to the *Calliope* we had plenty of room but that didn't prevent a lot of pushing. The Petty Officer was strutting about like a prize bantam cock, giving orders by the dozen, all of which seemed to me to go unheeded. Turning to face us, his chest six inches above normal and his face as red as the rising sun, he rasped out in a stentorian voice 'Party!' This meant that he was about to give us a further command so we had to pay attention. His lovely blue eyes searched the ranks to make sure that everyone agreed that he was now in sole command.

After considerable thought he decided we were all ears and screamed out 'Party, 'Shun'.

To the uninitiated, this means that you bring your left leg smartly against your right leg, closing your heels together with a click. You then stand perfectly still, stiff as a ram-rod, with head upright, chin in, chest out and stomach in. You are allowed to breathe but that is all. Eyes must look to the front and arms held closely to your sides with your thumbs in line with your trouser seams.

However perfectly this operation is carried out it is never done to the satisfaction of the man who has given the order and it has to be done over and over again, while the war waits.

Eventually the PO had his toy soldiers all nicely lined up and he rapped out his next order.

'From the right. Number!'

Now this is quite simple. The man on the extreme right of the line calls out in a clear voice 'One'. The man on his left calls 'Two' and so on down the line. Simple or not, the numbers got mixed up before they reached me and we started again.

When my turn came I called 'Fourteen' and my neighbour called 'Fifteen' but the numbering went astray again before reaching the end. Next time I was number thirteen; obviously someone had got fed up and gone home, leaving me with the unlucky number. It all seemed a lot of fuss but as I was not particularly delighted with 'thirteen' I really didn't mind when we began again. I tried to figure out the importance of this numbering business as the rear rank only had to remain silent The solution seemed easy – in future I would be in the rear rank. I was so busy solving my problem that I forgot we were engaged in this numbering game and didn't notice it was my turn to guess a number. The chap on my left appeared to be bent on pushing me out of the line altogether. I was not cross but I was forceful; nobody was going to push me out of the war. I had to do a bit of pushing but I managed to hold on to my bit of England.

The Petty Officer hurried towards me obviously to compliment me on my zeal. His face was much more coloured than I had previously noticed – inclined to blush it seemed. Still that was understandable; after all the chap I had sent sprawling was quite hefty.

'What's your monika?'he said quite firmly.

'Monika?' I asked in amazement 'I don't quite understand, – sir. I have not heard the expression before. Is it to do with my boxing abilities?'

'For your information, young man,' he said rather sweetly,

'its your name.'

'Oh,' I was quite relieved; I could see promotion in the air.

These fellows were a dense lot, anyway, unable even to call out a number.

With just pride and standing so erect that I almost fell over, the very first instruction given to me on board the *Calliope* came like a flash. 'Always give your full name.' So, very coolly and calmly I did just that.

'Is it, now? What a pretty name. And I suppose you are your mother's darling, aren't yer?'

I was rather inclined to agree with him about the pretty name, but somewhat doubtful about the 'darling'. Since he had inferred that I should confirm his surmise, I was about to explain when he bawled out 'Shut UP'. He explained in no uncertain manner that I was in the Navy now and not behind the plough – I was on the point of saying I already knew this but, just to remain friendly, I held my tongue. Already I had held up the parade and had spoiled all his efforts.

We ought to be somewhere else instead of messing about here. We had plenty to do and, through my having a private war of my own, I had almost lost the real war. I felt very sad, angry and full of remorse. I had delayed our march against the enemy but, consoling myself, war or no war no one was going to make a football of me.

It was now quite clear that the Petty Officer was of the opinion that I should have taken more notice of him than I did of the bully that started the shoving; I saw his point and left it at that.

Now that peace was re-established, the numbering was tried again and, strange to say, it was accomplished to the Petty Officer's entire satisfaction at the very first attempt I got rid of my thirteen; I was fourteen again and felt about the same age.

Further orders and instructions: Pay attention, there. On the command, form fours.' To achieve this the even numbers had to take a step to the rear on their left foot, then to the right with the right foot, bringing the left foot alongside the right. Now I knew why there was so much fuss about the numbering. The even ones had to do all the moving, and as my latest number was fourteen, I awaited the command with perfect confidence.

'Form' – rather slowly, a pause, and then 'Fours'.

What we should have done and what we did were vastly different. Some of the 'odds' moved when they should have remained still – I suppose they thought it was their duty to do something. To some of the others left was right which, of course, was wrong. Others started off on the wrong foot and did not have enough feet left to complete the movement; and the rest, ashamed that they were doing nothing to help in the war, began looking around for somewhere to go.

We had quite a few unsuccessful attempts but, try as we may, we could not get it right. It became increasingly clear to me that I would spend the rest of the war on the platform at King's Cross station, as the Petty Officer said he intended to 'have it done correctly' before we moved off. He kept his word but, in doing so, lost his temper and – strange to relate – never found it again.

Now we were ready to march to Berlin but, to our amazement, we only marched half-way down the platform and boarded the train standing there. 'We shall make a fresh start,' said the Petty Officer. It seemed to me to be a bit of a risk; we had been hours getting started and had only gone a matter of yards. We were ordered to alight and form up in two ranks facing the train.

'Form fours. Right turn. By the right, quick march!'

Off we went as if we had been doing it for years – along the Euston Road, down Tottenham Court Road, across Oxford Street into Charing Cross Road, along Shaftesbury Avenue, through Piccadilly to Hyde Park Corner and down Grosvenor Place to Victoria Station.

During the march we held up the traffic at every crossing and we. were given a clear passage throughout For some reason this pleased me – I think it made me feel important. It was nice to feel that the people of London appreciated that here in their midst was a bunch of lads that would prevent the Germans from invading England. This invasion idea was Tom's belief.

In his comments on the results of the Naval Manoeuvres in 1912 he wrote:

A foreign fleet escorting transports could land troops on the east coast of England between Sunderland and Cromer notwithstanding that a fleet comprising half as many battle-ships and cruisers over and above those of the invading fleet was patrolling the whole of the east coast.

Well, now we were at war with Germany and Tom was aboard the *Good Hope*. It was much too soon for the Germans to attempt a landing, but I held Tom's views and hoped that I would be thereabouts when they came. I pictured myself hidden on some high cliff overlooking a stretch of sand, with plenty of ammunition and comparatively safe. I could allow the invaders to actually land or pop them off by the score whilst they were still in their boats. Even though I was not yet trained, I fancied I could beat off an attack single-handed. At this year's Flower Show I had hit the balls off the top of the water jets and scored many 'bulls' too so surely I could hit a 'bull' six feet tall.

I thought when we began our march that I would have been fascinated by the tan buildings but after the first few minutes I became absorbed with my inner thoughts.

Boarding the tram at Victoria, we soon reached our destination, the Crystal Palace. We were immediately allocated to sleeping quarters. After a couple of days we were issued with sailors' uniforms, minus dickies, but this did not prevent the mad rush to the photographer's studio in Penge. This was a 'must' and the resulting works of art were duly sent home, later to find their way into the local papers.

I was never at any time proud of my features and longed to make a mess of the individual who sent my ghastly photograph to the Newcastle Leader.

My time at the Crystal Palace was spent in square-bashing and being bullied and pushed around all day. In the evening there was a few hours pleasure which made me forget all the troubles and trials of the day and the coming tomorrow. Outside the Palace we were idolized by the people of London but inside I doubt if the convicts in the ships going to Botany Bay suffered more humilities.

When, on October 31st, there was a call for volunteers to join the Hood, whatever that meant, I readily put up my hand and was warned to stand by for draft to Devonport Naval Barracks. This meant that I could not go ashore but had to remain within shouting distance. This did not unduly worry me as I would soon be on the move which was what I fervently desired.

The following night, November 1st, I found myself being searched upon entering the barracks at Devonport The inside of my hat was thoroughly examined in case it contained some secret weapon and then my only pocket. My matches were taken from me because they were not 'safety' matches and were thrown on the ground. I, with lots of others in the draft, had to pick them up before breakfast the following morning. This meant another meal lost as there was never anything left for those who were late. In fact there was never very much for those who were early. To rub it in, I was a defaulter and had to wash-up after the greedy hounds. All this because I had ordinary matches. I had never seen safety ones in my life; they would be useless in the mines anyway. Vulcan and Puck were the only matches I had ever had, Vulcan being the favourite because of their strong box. We live and learn.

Now that I was on draft I had to be frequently told the old story You're in the Navy now and not behind the plough'. I think this must be in King's Regulations as every Instructor uses it at the first possible opportunity. Personally I had never been behind the plough and was beginning to think that I was totally unsuited to serve behind the mast everything we knew we were told to forget We were no longer individuals with minds but numbered images without power of speech or reason. I was beginning to lose faith and it struck me forcibly that if I was to fight for my country I would have to fight myself first.

I had set off to fight the Germans because they had overrun Belgium, and if someone didn't stop them soon, they would overrun the whole of Europe. They had played havoc with the women and children in their advance to the Channel ports and they would do even worse, if that were possible, if they ever reached England. The object of my enlisting was to try to prevent them from succeeding but so far my intentions and ideals had been cast to the winds. I had been subjected to continuous insults and bullying. Were they trying to break my spirit? If so, they would be unlucky. I had set off to see this thing through and they could bully me as much as they liked. But why did they do it? Surely I could be trained to use a rifle or a bayonet without all this bullying. Was I such a numbskull? Could we all be daft? We were all hurried from morning till night and retired each night hoping that on the morrow things would be better.

In the Navy one rises early. I was quite used to early rising – up before the birds, feeling fit as a daisy and ready for the day's battle. One day it came in a different form and stopped me dead in my tracks. Everywhere I went there was talk of the loss with all hands of the *Good Hope* and the *Monmouth*.

I met many men who at some time in their service had been on those vessels. Everyone was most kind to me in my distress and I was grateful I tried to obtain some official confirmation but there was none forthcoming. I scribbled a short note telling my brother Eddie of the rumour, suggesting he should keep the sad news from Mother as maybe there would be some survivors. We must wait, but in my own mind I was in little doubt – the rumour was too strong. I wondered how Mother would take this tragic blow. We had all thought Tom was thousands of miles from danger and were pleased he was in the *Good Hope*. I was very worried and did not notice any bullying that day. My fed-up feeling had gone. I had a personal war now – I was no longer concerned with the Hun barbarities in Belgium.

In the Southern Pacific, off Coronel, Admiral Sir Christopher Cradock was engaged in playing tag with a squadron of the Imperial German Navy under Admiral von Spee. To play this game he had been allotted by the British Admiralty under Winston Churchill two obsolete cruisers. *Good Hope* and *Monmouth*; one light cruiser, the *Glasgow*; and one auxiliary, the ex-liner *Ontario*. All of these vessels were greatly inferior in fire power to their German counterparts, the cruisers *Scharnhorst. Gneisenau, Dresden, Leipzig* and *Nuremberg*. To redress the balance, the Admiralty then despatched the obsolete battleship *Canopus*, a slow vessel of only seventeen knots but considerably superior to the Germans in fire-power and range.

Cradock realised that at seventeen knots he had no hope of catching the German squadron. He therefore pushed on after the Germans without waiting for *Canopus*. When he did intercept the enemy, he did not shadow them until *Canopus*, less than twenty hours' sailing away, headed them off, out engaged them immediately notwithstanding his serious inferiority in gunpower and range. *Good Hope* and *Monmouth*, out-ranged and out-gunned, were sunk within the hour and one hundred years of invincibility since the battle of Trafalgar had gone to the bottom of the sea with them – and my brother.

An eye for an eye, a tooth for a tooth: this would be my motto from now on, come what may. I cared not for any instructors; they could bully, ridicule and scoff – I would not hear them. My object was quite clear in my mind. Tom was the eldest son and I the youngest. In the ordinary course of life the elder takes care of the younger but war upsets reason and routine. I worshipped him, though he did not know it. To me, everything he did was manly and honest There would come a time when I could avenge him.

For the moment I had temporary consolation. Mother did not know of the disaster and maybe there would be better news later on. Maybe the Good Hope had landed observation parties before the battle on some of the many remote islands. Maybe the Germans had picked up these observation parties or perhaps a few survivors. It might be months before we knew for certain; we must wait and hope for the best.

I had the feeling that Tom was not dead; it was so strong that I would like to have told Mother. So uncanny was the feeling that it was difficult to explain, but good news would come.

Time seemed to drag; I was doing the same things over and over again. I wanted to get to the fighting, wherever it might be, instead of this continual drilling and marching. Rumour had it that we were going to the rifle range at the end of the week and this gave me hope. My hopes were short-lived, however, as we went shooting with small-bore rifles on a thirty-yard range with six-inch cardboard squares for targets and the black o bulls about the size of a shilling. I was in the second batch. and had ample opportunity to note how easy it was to score bulls. The chap I was standing behind scored eight of ten shots. The remaining two were very close and were counted as 'inners'.

Lying full-length in front of the row of targets, my Marine instructor demonstrated how I should avoid dislocating my shoulder. I should hold the rifle firmly as the kick was severe and might smash my jaw if I held it loosely. 'All you have to do is to lie comfortably with feet pointing outwards and the heels pressing on the ground. Get the bull in line with the fore-sight and gently press, not pull, the trigger.'

It sounded quite clear and concise. I inwardly thanked him for his guidance and lay quite comfortably with the feet pointing outwards. Good heavens, how on earth could one be comfortable in this position? It was most uncomfortable and I adjusted my feet slightly. The instructor standing behind me instantly pressed my heel to the ground with his foot, upsetting my adjustment and my temper. My tummy ached as I waited for the signal to fire. I had had the bull in line with the foresight many times but just now I could see dozens of bulls prancing about. I raised my head to establish definitely which of these prancing bulls was on my target. Naturally, the signal to fire was given at that precise moment I hurriedly fired and the marker in the butts complained that someone was firing at him. Luckily he was protected by an iron shield which a short while ago I had thought quite unnecessary. On examining the targets they made the remarkable discovery that mine was undefiled. Well, I must have hit something! Lying in such a horrible position, it would not have surprised me if I had hit the sun.

After more kindly words of instruction I had another go, all by myself. I made myself as comfortable as was allowed with legs apart and feet pointing outwards.

'Don't wait for any signal. Fire when you get the bull in line with the foresight.' The accommodating bull appeared, as if by magic, dead in line. Full of confidence I pressed the trigger and could sec a hole right through the centre of the bull but upon closer inspection, it and the rest of the target remained unscathed. Even the butt-marker did not complain. The bullet had left my end but where it went we never found out.

I was getting worse. I had hit something the first go. To cut a long and tragic story short, I spent almost the whole day missing targets. If I did hit any, no one told me. It was a most disappointing day. If only they would let me lie comfortably I knew I could hit the bull.

What was worrying me was that when the time came for my crowd to go overseas they would leave me behind, it being safer.

I cannot attempt to put into words what the rest of the fellows said by way of encouragement – it would not make good reading. I would say, though, that men seem to find pleasure in other men's misfortunes. The general opinion was that I was trying to work my discharge and had suddenly got cold feet; I was the laughing stock of all and sundry.

I had come to this crowd to help to defeat a common enemy, but it looked as though I would have to begin my battle here in England. I can enjoy a joke with the rest but some of those crack-shots were positively insulting. I determined not to stand much more of their nonsense.

The days seemed to pass a little more quickly and drilling and route-marching took up most of the time. Physical training was very popular and lots of the lads threw their weight about. They all fancied that they were clever with their fists and each evening in the Block's basement there was boxing, It was a real slaughter-house at times but we all enjoyed it. I was satisfied to stand and watch until one night when one of the clever boys, who was bashing his opponent about the ring, saw me watching him. and from then onwards he amused the crowd by likening his opponent's punches to my shooting – not very effective, a little wide and off the target. After his bout he suggested he would like to give me a lesson in straight-shooting. I, to the crowd's obvious delight, accepted the challenge, I fooled about for the first round until I got the measure of him. When the bell went for the second round I set about him in earnest. I clouted him unmercifully. A lovely upper-cut to his chin lifted him clean off the floor and that was that.

Would any of you other sharp-shooters like to show me how to box?' There were no offers. It was surprising the effect this one fight had on the innuendoes that had been flying about. A few days later we had to do some real shooting with ball cartridges. We had to fire across a stretch of water and the targets seemed miles away; actually our first target was at 300 yards. Strange to say, I was not the least bit nervous. I knew in my own mind that it. I was to go overseas I had to hit those targets and I knew that I could. I simply cannot understand what went wrong at the small-bore range; maybe I was expecting more kick than there really was. I knew that these proper rifles would kick. I was in the first batch to fire and fancied the absence of a waiting period would be to my advantage. My first round was signalled as a bull and I wondered if it really was my shot. Maybe someone was firing at the wrong target, quite a common error on the ranges. My second shot was an inner and the third another bull. Of course I could shoot now as I had the feel of my rifle and I would shoot anyone who said I could not.

We fired ten rounds at 300 yards, ten rounds at 500 yards and another ten rounds at 700 yards. At this latter distance I was top scorer in my section but on the aggregate I tied for third place and I was more than satisfied. As usual, it rained the whole day; no sooner had we boarded the tender to go to the butts when down came the rain. We had five days'shooting and five days downpour. I have never met anyone who did their firing in dry weather. The inclement weather had not bothered me as I knew I would not be left behind when the time came for service overseas.

One evening towards the end of November 1914 all leave was cancelled. Rifles and full equipment were issued and we were stood by to move off at a moment's notice – destination unknown. This meant that we could not turn in or even remove our boots. The lads played cards all night and Tubby and I talked as usual. Nice fellow, Tubby; we could always find something of mutual interest to talk about.

As darkness vanished, so did our hopes. We had expected to leave during the night and some had written to their folks saying they were about to leave for active service.

Instead, we handed in our equipment and returned to normal until December, 5th, when the whole Hood Battalion moved to Blandford in Dorset. Some desk-bound War Office General had, out of sheer spite, decided that we should be spirited away to the most isolated wilderness in the country. The exact location was about three miles from the small old-world town. A few huts had been erected but they had forgotten to make a road to them.

Within an hour of our arrival the space between the huts was a quagmire. Some of the huts were only partially complete, but we had them ship-shape in a few days and we soon settled down to camp life. We collected our three boards and two trestles and there was plenty of straw to be had to fill our palliasses. Issued with two blankets each, we were supposed, to be comfortable, but we nearly froze to death.

We were out on the downs all day training. If it rained – and it usually did – we got wet and plastered with mud and chalk and were expected to get dried out the best way we could. No one ever thought of building drying rooms. We had one small oil heater in each hut which gave off less heat than a miner's lamp.

Still it was an open-air life and the healthy, invigorating Dorset air was just what we needed to make us fighting fit; only the fit survived.

When the day's trials were over we made our way across the muddy Downs and then through a small wood until we reached the road that led to the town. This was out of bounds after eight o'clock in the evening and as soon as you neared the town you were pounced upon by the Military Police and ordered to produce your permit. In fact we spent most of the evening producing permits. The Military Police were pests; they just would not leave us alone. It got so bad that most of us preferred to sit in the gloomy hut all evening.

The last time I went to town I was pulled up and reported. I pointed out that it was only four minutes to eight. The MP agreed but said I could not get to the boundary in four minutes.

'Not if you hold me here,' I said. This was added to the charge when it was read out the next morning by Sergeant-Major Paddy Hynn. The seriousness of my offence was outlined. I had committed a book full of crimes but I was young and inexperienced – the punishment: admonishment.

Some days later, our route-march across the Downs brought us to a small village called Pimpeme. From there we marched along the road that passed through Blandford. Until then few of us had known of the existence of this road and it gave us the idea to use this route when next we went to town. It would take longer but if the weather were reasonable we would be able to keep ourselves fairly respectable. On trying this new way, however, we found the old enemy even more active. The redcaps found fault with the angles of our caps, as they found fault with everything, so we reverted to the old muddy track through the wood.

In this time and age, 1914, no two watches ever told the same time and there was constant arguing as to which one was correct. In all probability they were all wrong. In my little band one chap had his Dad's, lent for the duration; it was at least thirty years old and had been in the pawnshop as many times. Another was a birthday gift from Auntie Flo and required winding every half-hour. Tubby's would only go when lying on its face. Mine was an English lever. Tom gave it to me when we visited him on board HMS *Ocean* lying at Rosyth. I was called in on many occasions to settle an argument about the correct time.

Of course the redcaps had their own time. If they said it was midnight, then it was midnight, even though the sun had not yet set. I have heard of the midnight sun In the far north but even the arctic conditions in the camp did not convince me that my geography was that much at fault.

When being escorted back to camp through the wood, there were times when the escort had the shocking misfortune to trip himself up, causing the prisoner to come in contact with his ugly face. The nose was somehow the usual point of contact The prisoner, alarmed at the flow of blood and fearing that the chap might bleed to death, would then hop off quickly to get first aid. On arrival at the camp, though, he was so short of breath himself that he had to rest awhile on his own bed. During this resting period it was customary for the casualty to arrive with the duty Petty Officer, looking for the chap who, at great personal risk, had volunteered to bring aid. I suppose he desired to thank him for his noble effort but, if he was present, the modest chap kept quiet It was a waste of time looking for the hero, anyway. Only an hour ago the Petty Officer himself had called the roll and distinctly heard everyone answer his name and had reported all present to the Orderly Officer.

A few days later a working party arrived from the Crystal Palace and all the joys, misfortunes and anomalies that arise in the erection of a new camp were handed over to these men. They built a splendid new road from Blandford to a hospital in the making and named it Hospital Lane.

We now began field training in earnest, marching all day and – often all night. The rainy season set in and turned the Downs into one huge expanse of mud. We trudged through this mud looking for an enemy we never found, but kept on looking. When we came to a nice watery patch we would be ordered to lie down, taking particular care to keep. the head down in case the enemy were about.

The end of the year was drawing near. We wallowed in the mud all day and cleaned up all night ready for the morrow's mud bath. Each and every day was more or less the same old routine, but Christmas was coming and we hoped for a few days leave.

The camp broke up on December 23rd, 1914. All were granted six days' leave. I was a little homesick; I wanted to Visit my home and my people and lost no time in getting away from the quagmire.

Upon arriving is Newcastle I found I had a couple of hours to wait for the first train to Lintz Green. Tom had always visited Uncle Bill and Aunt Maggie over in Gateshead, so I o did the same – much to my regret. They were asleep when I knocked and presently Aunt Maggie came to the door. Seeing me standing there clad in sailor's uniform, in the darkness she thought it was Tom and collapsed in my arms. I was sorry that I had barged in on them in this way, but there had been no way of letting them know. Of course they made me welcome. I would never have heard the last of it if I had not called, as Tom always called.

The late night tram from London invariably arrived-in Newcastle too early for the first train to Lintz Green. It was the other way round on the return journey, the local tram arriving two hours earlier than the departure time of the London train. Tom would never have dreamed of going back without visiting Uncle and Aunt. Now I had taken his place I would do as he did, but I, too, was upset. I was afraid to go home, and the words of the poet, John Moultrie, were ringing in my ears:

I loved my home but trembled now.
To view my father's altered brow;
I feared to meet my mother's eye
And hear her voice of agony.

I had remained in Gateshead much longer than I originally intended but managed to arrive home quite early in the morning. My uniform made things very awkward, so as soon as I got the greetings over and had the inevitable cup of tea with Mother, I changed into my civilian clothes. I was thus attired, when I met Father and the lads. I rather thought they would have preferred to see me to uniform, but they understood.

My whole holiday was spent without looking once at my bell-bottomed trousers.

The time to go back soon came, so, with my bundle under my arm, I kissed Mother good-bye and told her not to worry. Pear old Mrs Ellis from next door was already with Mother, so I again took my leave and, as before, I turned to wave to her before turning the corner at the end of the street. I soon caught up with the party. Geordie with his concertina had them all singing. We arrived at Lintz Green station in sufficient time to conclude the kissing and hand-shaking before the train arrived, so, off to a flying-start, we – Father, brothers and sisters and I – were soon to Gateshead.

Uncle Bill nearly had a fit when he saw that I was going back to camp in civilian clothes. Again the inevitable cup of tea.

Five minutes' walk to the High Level Bridge and a half-penny ride on the brake took us over the bridge. Once on the other side, seven or eight minutes' walk took us to the Central Station. I presented my sailor's warrant at the barrier; the ticket inspector was not at all convinced with my explanation that my uniform had been soiled just before leaving home and that I had it in the parcel under my arm. He said I could have found the warrant and told me I would have to report to the Railway Transport Officer at the far end of the station. If I had acted on this advice I would have gone back to Blandford under escort, as civilian clothes were not allowed.

Uncle Bill took hold of my arm, saying: 'Come along and do as the Inspector says.' We wandered off until out of the Inspector's sight, with the rest of the party following, but instead of heading for the RT Office, Uncle Bill led the party to the other barrier. With a broad grin he produced a handful of platform tickets which were accepted without their even being counted.

I claimed a corner seat to the tram by putting my parcel down. A few minutes later the tram was on its way to London and I made my way to the end of the coach. I reappeared in the compartment before the tram reached Durham, as a fully rigged sailor. When, in a most casual way, I took my corner seat, I was told quite politely that the seat was already taken by a civilian chap who had gone out for a few moments. I said I knew the chap very well and he would not mind my taking his seat; in fact a few moments ago I was a civilian myself. Some minutes elapsed before they saw the joke,

The journey to King's Cross was uneventful; most of the chaps were returning to Portsmouth and no one had even heard of Blandford.

'What sort of a ship is she?'

She's the latest addition to the Home Fleet, flat-bottomed and unsinkable; a real stick-in-the-mud and sister ship to HMS *Crystal Palace*.' With that, we parted to go our various ways. I had quite a long time to wait for the train to Templecombe that would connect with the Blandford train. I was studying a map of the Underground when I got into conversation with a Cockney. He was very helpful and insisted on my having something to eat with him. I enjoyed the lunch and his company. He saw me to the station and I was sorry when, on the platform, we had to say goodbye.

It was late at night when I alighted from the train at Blandford. It had been a long and tiresome journey and there was still that miserable three-mile walk to the camp, during which I had ample time to sort myself out.

I had enjoyed my leave and wondered if I had done and said the right things. I must have awakened my memories – the comings and goings of Tom that would never be repeated. Was it humanly possible for one to be happy and sad at the same tune? What a dilemma for Mother and what agonising thoughts she must have had; her youngest son leaving and her eldest never to return. I had not realised what a great woman she really was. All the silly things that I had done in the past that had annoyed her came back to me with full force. I felt thoroughly ashamed of myself and vowed that never again would I say or do, or even think of doing, anything that would cause her the slightest distress. With these thoughts I finally went off to sleep and with the dawn came the end of 1914.

Three months had passed since my enlistment and the war was still raging. Here I was playing soldiers, but clad in a sailor's uniform. Almost everyone had thought the war would have fizzled out by now and that three months was the absolute limit. How wrong could one be? If it took as long to train a German recruit as it was obviously going to take to train us, the war would go on forever.

New Year's Day: no training, but we made up for it the following day. We marched anywhere and everywhere, stopping now and then to do bayonet practice – naval style, of course. Then more marching and squad drill – 'Right wheel left wheel, on the left form platoon, right incline, left incline, about turn, halt, order arms, slope arms, by the right quick march.' It was heartbreaking. The same movements over and over again all day and every day. Rushing here and there, lying down in the mud and then standing in the freezing wind and rain, it all appeared to be so useless. Was it an attempt disguised under a doubtful interpretation of the word 'discipline' to break our spirit? Be that as it may, that was how the days and weeks were spent.

We had become accustomed to Service food and the open-air life was doing us good. Our health was excellent and we were a happy crowd.

CHAPTER TWO

JANUARY

Friday, January 8th, 1915

We were inspected by Mr Winston Churchill on the part of the Downs known as Three Mile Point.

Friday, January 15th

Inspected by His Majesty King George V, accompanied by Mr Churchill This was most satisfying as it conveyed to those who understood procedure that this was the final inspection before we proceeded overseas. After the parade Chief Petty Officer Milton told us we were destined to force the Dardanelles and that we would be leaving almost at once. This was to keeping with the original intention of forming the Naval Brigades.

The following day I wrote to my people and told them the news. In due course they replied. They were exceedingly pleased with the news and were of the opinion that I was very fortunate to be going to the Mediterranean. I would miss the slaughter that was going on to France and it would be more of a sightseeing tour.

We had to be dressed for the occasion, We discarded our blue sailors' uniforms and were Issued with soldiers' uniforms, I did see one or two men in khaki sailors' rig-out but this style was apparently not suitable for the job in hand. We did, however, retain our Naval-style cap, but khaki in colour, with a black cap-band bearing the battalion's name in gold lettering. Later we were issued with pith helmets which looked awfully naked without their puggarees. A puggaree is a long strip of muslin, about two inches wide, which must be neatly folded round the outside of the helmet This is much more easily said than done.

I spent days trying to get this confounded strip to look even respectable. It was almost worn out before it passed the examination of my Platoon Officer, Sub-Lieutenant Arthur Asquith.

The change of uniform did not alter our Naval status. We held on to our naval ratings, but the training was purely military. Each day it became more arduous, which was to be accepted and expected.

By now the camp was beginning to get quite homely and footpaths between the huts made it possible to do a spot of local visiting. The canteen was very helpful in making up the vast deficiencies to our menu. A go-as-you-please concert was held almost every night We had a silver band when out marching and a mouth-organ band to the canteen. I think the latter was most preferred.

The old soldiers said that when we got among the fighting we would have to sleep in our uniforms. The huts were so cold that quite a few of us had been doing this for some time. Apart from the warmth it saved such a lot of time to the morning, especially in getting to the breakfast table. There was plenty to eat if you were not particular what you ate, but you had to be quick. We would be on our way soon and that was all that mattered.

'The days came and went and every day had its quota of rumours: 'Leaving at the end of the week' – 'Operation cancelled' – 'Going to France after all'. Each rumour was said to come from an impeccable source. Camp life in England was – like the month – drawing to a close and, looking back on it, it had not been so bad really.

CHAPTER THREE

FEBRUARY

Saturday, February 27th

Dies datus. A truly appointed day, ever to be remembered. We paraded wearing our recently acquired sun helmets even though it was pouring with rain. At six in the evening, Lieutenant-Colonel Quilter gave the order we had waited for months to hear.

'The Battalion will move off in column of route, 'A' Company leading.' Without the slightest fuss the battalion moved off. We had expected to entrain at Blandford but after two hours march in a heavy downpour, we arrived at Shillingstone and boarded the waiting tram. We were soaked to the skin but very happy indeed.

Sunday, February 28th

At three in the morning we arrived alongside the *Grantully Castle*, a vessel of 7,592 tons, lying at Avonmouth. When we had eventually loaded our equipment we received orders to stay aboard. To make sure that we did so, sentries were placed at the head of the gangway.

We had ample promenade space, but the sleeping quarters appeared to be hopelessly inadequate. It seemed an impossibility for us all to sling our hammocks in the area allotted to sleeping, but we succeeded.

We had more or less got settled down when another train drew up alongside bringing the Anson batallion. Like us, they had quite a lot of stuff to hump aboard before finally settling down. Our hopes of plenty of room had unmercifully departed with the coming of an additional 1,000 men. I was pleased to meet a pal of mine among the newcomers – Armitage Jewitt – who had lived only four doors away from me at home. We saw quite a lot of each other during our voyage to the Middle East.

Less than twenty-four hours after leaving Blandford, the mooring lines were cast off and we moved slowly away from England, leaving less than a dozen on the quayside to wave us *bon voyage*. What had Fate in store for us? If we could have looked forward, say four years or so, how many of us would have fallen from the path we were now taking. How many were to return? Maybe it is mericiful not to see too far ahead.

Sailing down the Bristol Channel as the sun was setting was a thrilling experience. I had noticed the sunsets of late; they had been sombre with troubled skies but this night's sunset. I would be forever remembered because for me it was the first of a new era. I was leaving with a nasty task to do and my heart was heavy.

Travellers and poets have in truth and fiction described their feelings on leaving their homeland but it is sufficient to say that neither traveller nor poet can adequately describe the parting. The sky had been beautiful all day. Now, a tremendously long light-pink and orange cloud lay across its soft blue vault and pale mauve clouds floated above the horizon, only to suddenly change to red and orange surmounted by soft saffron, as the sun sank.

As I watched, I longed to have been an artist to portray adequately a scene so vivid and so real. Awed by the beauty of such surroundings I thought that if the gates of Paradise could be more beautiful or more supendous than this earthly sunset, I hoped that at some future date I might make acquaintance with them. It is usually agreed, however, that the life of a soldier practically annuls all such heavenly anticipations.

A bugle call brought me back to earth with a bump. We appeared to be clear of the Bristol Channel. Our escort of five destroyers was continually signalling and coming in quite close. How gracefully these vessels cut the sea and how neat they looked compared with the five transports in the convoy. The lights of England were sinking out of view – for how long, I wondered.

The stiff breeze forced me to go below, with the idea of turning to, but the stench nauseated me. Collier, an old merchant seaman from Liverpool, was bawling at the top of his voice 'Land ahead!' and pointing to his dirty feet sticking out from the end of his hammock. I found my own hammock and carried it back on deck. Someone had borrowed my blankets so, with the hammock as my only covering, I slept on deck until awakened by the crew, who thought it funny to turn upon us the three-inch hoses they were using to wash the deck.

I had slept reasonably well but did not feel so good when I began to walk about. The sea was choppy and the old ship could not make up her mind whether to go over the huge waves or underneath them. She often appeared to be going sideways, with the result that most of us youngsters spent the early hours looking over the port rail one moment and the starboard rail the next I suppose the Skipper made the usual note in the log book: *Ship holding on course.* I was more concerned in holding on to my breakfast, but the sea, that choppy, hungry sea, claimed it.

The mess orderlies of the day had to negotiate almost perpendicular open ladders whilst carrying trays of skilly, a highly 'skilful' operation in calm weather, let alone foul. Many of the huge trays of this ghastly stuff reached the lower deck long before their carriers. At other times both came unceremoniously down together. If they were still attached to one another and the orderly managed to wade through the slippery mess at the foot of the ladder, those that still desired to eat – there were not many could help themselves.

Our rations were one slice of bread each and a small rasher of the vilest salty bacon I had ever seen, followed by a basin of what the cooks called 'tea', all this provided the orderly had managed to keep his balance and his dixie. Those of us who had money joined the queue at the small cabin amidships that served as a canteen, hoping to buy something more palatable to eat. After about an hour I had not reached the serving hatch when the bugle sounded for parade, so breakfast was over.

Hood Battalion paraded on one side of the ship and Anson on the other. We had a little physical training and rifle drill – nothing strenuous – which was appreciated by all. We were out of sight of land; I felt out of this world but I was not the only one.

When parade was over I was not very anxious about dinner, but went below nevertheless. One fleeting glance at the mutton stew, to be followed by off-white rice, was enough. I took my place in the canteen queue again. This time I was in luck's way – three biscuits and a morsel of cheese, all for the price of threepence, and a cup (if you had yours with you) of tea for twopence.

Another bugle call and another parade. Afterwards we had our final meal of the day – one slice of bread with a little jam, washed down with a basin of tea. The evening, like the lovely sunset, was free for card playing, housey-housey, crown and anchor, letter-writing and meditation. So ended our first full day at sea.

As on the first night, Armitage Jewitt, Tubby and I took up our spot on the deck and slept quite peacefully until rudely awakened by the deck washers. The weather was foul with huge seas running. The old ship was trying her utmost to pitch the lot of us into the sea. One minute I was looking into the sea, almost touching it, and the next I was gazing into the sky. The pitching and rolling and all the other antics continued all day and night and for most of the next day. It was not until late evening of the third day that the old tub got back on an even keel.

The lights on the Spanish coast could easily be seen. The crew said they were on Cap Finisterre. The following day we kept close in as we steamed along the coast of Portugal. The weather was now quite respectable and much warmer than the previous day's.

Despite the lack of food, I felt fine. It must have been the sea air and the biscuits and cheese, plus an occasional mug of cocoa bought from the crew late at night. This additional mug of concentrated vitamins was not allowed as we might get too fat; if caught, it meant more fatigues.

CHAPTER FOUR

MARCH

Friday, March 5th

I had arranged for one of the crew to give me a kick when we entered the Straits of Gibraltar as I longed to see the Rock. Tom had told me so much about it that I felt sure I could find my way about if at any time I landed there. It was three o'clock in the morning and, though quite dark, I could see its outline. How I longed for the sun to rise so that I could see it clearly; maybe we should pass through the Straits in daylight on our return journey but I had seen the Rock and was satisfied.

The weather was glorious with a warm sun and the sea calm as a mill-pond. It was good to be alive and I had become accustomed to the frugal diet We kept-close in to the African coast and the voyage was now very interesting. I knew my geography well and realised that the first large town would be Oran and that we might see it late tonight if we went full steam ahead, both knots. There was quite a lot of shipping about.

Saturday, March 6th

After the usual hearty breakfast we paraded on deck, as on previous days, but without rifles. We were ordered: 'Off tunics and roll up the left shirt sleeves.' The Medical Officer appeared with his bag of tricks and we were vaccinated in turn on the bared left arm – this would not interfere with our rifle drill. Most of us were all right the following morning except for a little soreness, but some, happily not many, were really ill and confined to their hammocks for several days.

We were still close to the African coast, with the grim Atlas Mountains overshadowing the landscape. We passed Algiers and Bizerta, then rounded Cape Bon and thus down to Malta.

Monday, March 8th

At three o'clock in the afternoon we anchored in the Grand Harbour, followed by two French warships. Our silver band struck up *The Marsellaise*, followed by God Save the King – Our entire ship's company and the crews of both French warships stood to attention until the band finished playing, then everyone cheered loudly and waved his hat. It was a rousing welcome.

My Company Commander, Lieutenant-Commander Parsons, to whom I had confided my brother's service with the Navy and of his being aboard the Good Hope, told me to report to him in half-an-hour. He took me ashore with him, and after making one or two small purchases, gave them to me to take back on board.

Mind you get aboard before 'Lights Out' and report to me before parade in the morning,' he said, as we set off in opposite directions.

Where I went I have not the faintest idea. I certainly had a good look round and got back on board, as instructed, just before 'Lights Out'. In the morning I handed over the two packages to Commander Parsons and at the same time I thanked him for taking me ashore. I could not find words adequate enough to convey my heartfelt thanks; I think he knew.

Tuesday, March 9th

We steamed out of the Grand Harbour at eleven o'clock in the morning and did not see land until the following afternoon when we reached the Cyclades, those hundreds of islands that lie between the Mediterranean and the Aegean. What an ideal hiding place for submarines. I hoped there were none about!

Thursday, March 11th

Arrived at the island of Lemnos; we were now less than fifty miles from the Dardanelles. It was late afternoon when we steamed into Mudros

Harbour, our course lying between the *Queen Elizabeth* and the *Lord Nelson*. The harbour was full of warships, old and new. The *Lizzie* was the newest and the most powerful of them all and her presence here with us was a tonic. Also at Mudros was the Dreadnought Inflexible and the cruisers *Triumph* and *Swiftsure*, built in England for Turkey at the time of the Russo-Japanese War but not delivered in order to prevent Russia from buying them. They were lying along-side the very ship they were originally intended to sink if they got half a chance, the Russian cruiser *Askold*, promptly nick-named 'Woodbine' because of her five slender funnels. Still more warships, the *Asamemnon*, *Cornwallis*, *Implacable*, *London*, *Bacchante*, *Doris* and *Minerva* and the French battleships *Charlemagne*, *Suffren* and *Henri IV* – this ship by the look of her was built during Henri IVs reign and she had the appearance and style of a castle afloat. Her freeboard astern appeared to be almost awash, her turrets high above the water and her towers higher still. Also at anchor were many destroyers, torpedo craft, submarines, repair and depot ships; together with transports from all parts of the world.

We remained on board all day on Friday but on Saturday both Hood and Anson battalions were ashore all day, skirmishing and marching.

Time had stood still on this island; I observed a Greek using a wooden plough drawn by two oxen and making a really good furrow, but the pace was slow.

It was nice to be on dry land again; one felt more free and able to move about. Somehow the air was different and the sun was hot. There was no shade anywhere.

Each day the routine was much to the pattern of the first day. We went over the side by way of rope ladders and into the ships' boats – rowed ourselves ashore, scrambled out and lined the beach to attack the mythical enemy. After we had cleared the beach we got back into some sort of formation and marched inland, followed by supposedly friendly Greek inhabitants offering for sale chocolate, oranges and figs. This was comical as neither oranges nor figs grew on the island; they must have been brought from the Turkish mainland. We were supposed to be a secret army and were fooling about on an island only some forty-seven miles from the Dardanelles, whilst some of the inhabitants were obviously in contact with either Greece or Asia Minor.

Thursday, March 18th

Recalled from the island and within an hour – at six o'clock in the evening – were steaming out of Mudros Harbour. A cool breeze was blowing as we steered an easterly course for a little while and then veered to the north. We were on our way to the Dardanelles – action at last!

We were all very excited; although no orders had been given, we knew that Russia was desperately short of war materials but had ample grain, whilst the Western Allies had arms to spare but were short of foodstuffs. Our task would be to force the Dardanelles so that an exchange could be made.

Friday, March 19th

Arrived in the Gulf of Xeros (Saros) at five-thirty in the morning. As we steamed slowly down the western coast of the Gallipoli Peninsula, we were ordered to man the rails in full battle order, which we did, our bayonets glistening in the sun.

We were close inshore and about to land. Some of the men were pointing out the cliffs where they said they could see Turks, but although I peered hard I could not see anyone for certain.

HMS Dublin seemed to be escorting us towards the entrance to the Straits. The *Queen Elizabeth* was bombarding the shore and destroyers were cruising round and round. Many ships were firing and great clouds of smoke stretched across the whole area.

As we arrived at the entrance to the most famous straits in the world, many more warships came into view, each firing at its own target, the destroyers and torpedo craft continuing to circle.

In full view of the Turks, we expected the order to disembark at any moment but the order was not to be given this day. For two hours we remained on view, watching and wondering. No doubt the Turks were also wondering exactly where and when we would strike; as invaders it was for us to choose the time and place. There was not much choice of landing place but, even so, the decision was ours. The Turks had to remain where they were, ready to defend their homeland.

Our warships had been shelling the coastal forts for months and demolition parties had landed at Sedd el Bahr and Kum Kale two weeks ago. Thus the Turks had received ample warning and no doubt were ready, nicely hidden in and on top of those high cliffs.

We had come over two thousand miles, opened the gate and strolled up the garden path. The door stood wide open but we did not enter but turned and left.

Twenty hours after leaving Mudros we again anchored in the harbour. The naval attack on the Straits had failed. We had lost three ships – the

Ocean, Irresistible and *Bouvet* – and *Infexible* was badly holed, not by gunfire but all by mines. The channel had been swept again and again; whether the sweepers had missed these mines, or whether they were free and coming down with the current, we did not know but it was clear that so long as the Turks held the banks of the Straits, mines would always be a menace.

The Gallipoli Peninsula must be occupied but the Navy could not go it alone.

Wednesday, March 24th

After two weeks stay at Mudros, at six o'clock in the evening we sailed for Egypt. Rumour was that the Navy had abandoned the idea of forcing the Straits alone; it would have to be a joint affair with the Army. Apparently all our transports were not loaded to suit this new proposition and we were going to Egypt so that this could be rectified.

The following day we each received Princess Mary's Christmas Gift, a small, neat brass box containing a pipe, a little tobacco, cigarettes and a piece of chocolate or toffee.

Saturday. March 27th

Arrived at Port Said at seven o'clock in the morning. My platoon, the 9th 'C' Company, went ashore almost at once as a general working party, setting up tents to form our camp. This was not so easy as one would expect as the tent poles had to be in a perfectly straight line.

'A little to the right – much too far – back a little – more – more – hold it up straight – that's it – hold it!'

Thus each pole had to be moved this way and that for what seemed to be hours. Even when we managed to get our line correct it was not in alignment with the other lines; and so it went on all the afternoon. It was late in the evening before the tents were finally erected.

Sunday, March 28th

The Hood Battalion disembarked from the *Grantully Castle* and marched to the camp on the sands just outside the town. However ridiculous it may seem, there were twenty-seven men allocated to my tent. A dozen at the most could get inside an ordinary bell tent so the remainder had to sleep outside. During the day it was extremely hot but after sundown it was quite cold.

The following day we began light training. The days start early in the

East but all parades were over before four in the afternoon, leaving the evening free.

We were allowed into town until eight each evening, but were strongly advised not to go into the Arab Quarter, Of course, once in the town everyone made a bee-line for the Arab Quarter and most of the night was occupied in dodging our dear friends, the redcaps. This was easy among the narrow alleys as every door was open to a soldier and Welcome written on every mat So long as you had money you had plenty of doubtful company and were well out of reach of the Military Police, who maintained that the Arab Quarter was out of bounds. As I have said before, they were always right and it was we who had not heard the instruction correctly.

Each day our route march took us through this quarter, Marching was extremely arduous in the heat and on the soft sand. We were soon fatigued and, as a result, were ordered to cut our trousers to knee length. Scissors were not issued as part of a soldier kit so we had to make do with our jack knives. These knives are all right for opening jam tins but for tailoring they are far from ideal. However, the order was to cut, so cut we did! The first leg – apart from the jagged edges – was no problem but to get the other leg the same length was quite a poser and a sight not to be missed even in Egypt. The trousers were laid on the sand, the owner on his knees and with his nakedness exposed to the burning sun, endeavouring to make both legs equal before hacking off the unwanted part. To the passer-by – and there were many – the scene must have resembled a group of ardent pilgrims offering up prayers, but we had a job to do. Having made the cut, the trousers then had to be tried on; then a little more off the outside of the left leg and another fitting. Now a bit too much – what a pity – this meant a little bit off the right leg. So the hacking went on until some of the chaps had not much left of either leg.

On parade next day, some of us looked very rude, cooler in the body perhaps but looking rather hot in the face. At the end of the day our legs were just pieces of raw meat, the sand and sweat and the constant chafing causing excruciating pain. It had been our custom to have a dip in the canal before breakfast but we had to forgo this treat for a couple of days.

The canal was an ideal spot for those of us who could swim.

There was a gradual slope for about a yard and then at least-ten feet of water. We would run down the slope to the water and then dive in.

One of my section, George Packwood, was an expert swimmer and also an expert at fooling about; always up to his larks, he could see a joke in everything; Once he took four of us from the camp at Blandford to Bournemouth by hired car. Unfortunately, just after we left the camp we came across an old man who always turned his back when he saw soldiers. If we were on the march he would stand in the hedge with his back towards us. We took a poor view of this insult and threw all sorts of things at him as we passed but the officer soon got wise to this and would stand by the old man until the column was clear.

On this particular day George was in control and the moment he spotted the old man he drove straight in his direction, sounding the hooter incessantly. The old man realised the car was on the grass verge after him and he ran! The faster he ran, the faster the car came. He then rushed through a gap in the hedge but that did not stop George. When the old man was exhausted, George decided that was enough for the day. He shot across the field, through the gap and on to Bournemouth.

To get back to the canal, George would swim out, wave his arms and splash about and then call for help. We would all swim out to him but, when we reached him, he would dive under us and grab our feet. Today, however, he did not swim out; he dived and immediately cried for help. We went to his aid but – to teach him a lesson – on reaching him threw him into deep water. Poor old George, though, genuinely appeared to be in trouble so we dived in and hauled him out. When we laid him on the warm sand he said that his legs were very cold. I tucked my tunic round him but he still complained of the cold. Someone brought a stretcher and George, the heart and soul of the section, was carried to hospital to die with a broken spine.

CHAPTER FIVE

APRIL

Saturday, April 3rd

We were inspected by Sir Ian Hamilton on the sands just outside the camp. Immediately after the march-past we had to break step as the sands began to roll like the waves of the sea. It was like trying to walk on a spring mattress,

The Anson Battalion left at once for Alexandria. They were to 'act as a working party for the 9th Division who had apparently just arrived. Like us, their transports had to be reloaded to suit the job on hand.

Easter Sunday, April 4th

Out and about very early in the morning doing a little firing practice. We placed six-inch square tiles along the bank of the canal for use as targets. During the firing a muezzin could be heard calling to the faithful from a minaret in the town. I'm afraid the muezzin's call to prayer this morning was not heeded as most of the people were watching us, panic stricken. I think they thought the Turkish army was on the other side of the canal. They are normally extremely garrulous and Bedlam, compared to a mob of excited Arabs, would be a Victorian tea-party. Long after we had finished firing they were still highly excited and looking very worried. Incidentally, the Turks did attack the canal three days later but were beaten off. Our composite force at El Kantara was not in any way troubled.

Friday April 9th

Another chap in my section died in the town hospital, Dai Aston, one of the four Welshmen with us. He was a quiet, reserved sort of person. He appeared to be quite fit and well when we came ashore less than two weeks ago.

My section seemed to be having a run of bad luck. Those who were left were detailed as the firing party at his funeral in the local cemetery. As we approached the burial ground, our solemn procession was overtaken by an Arab funeral. Our slow march with arms reversed contrasted sharply with the singing, shouting and laughing Arab bearers who held their bier shoulder high. Again and again they lifted the corpse high above their heads. The chimney arrangement at the head sway-ing sideways to an alarming degree, they trotted along, followed by several low mule-drawn carts laden with the paid mourners who were sitting cross-legged and dressed in black, complete with veil and yashmak. They were the only sign of reverence in the whole procession.

It is customary for blank cartridges to be used by a firing party but, as we were on active service, blanks were not available and we had to use live ammunition. Instead of firing from both sides of the grave; we took up a position on the land side so that the spent bullets would fall into the sea out of harm's way. This meant that we were facing the Arab burial party and would fire over their heads. The first volley caused them to drop the coffin and flee in panic.

After the funeral we struck camp and boarded the *Grantully Castle* again and were ready to sail.

Saturday, April 10th

Early in the morning, with a cool refreshing breeze blowing, we steamed towards the open sea on our way back to the Dardenelles, knowing full well that our reception would not be so peaceful as on our last visit. The element of surprise – so essential for this sort of enterprise – had been lost long ago. Still, we were young and thirsting for adventure and were not unduly worried. In fact, we were eagerly looking forward to our new adventure.

As we steamed slowly past de Lessep's monument at the entrance to the canal, I reflected that his works were of construction whereas ours would be of destruction – human and material. His name would live for ever; how soon would ours be forgotten? Time would tell.

Once clear of the breakwater, the sea was rough and gradually got worse. The storm reached its peak on the thirteenth when we lost the lighter we were towing. We picked it up on the following day when the sea had become much calmer. We then proceeded on our way to the island of Lemnos.

Thursday, April 15th

A fancy dress ball was held in the late afternoon. The most original costumes were to be seen. I was astonished to find myself gazing at a young 'lady' clad in the finest coloured silks, looking very seductive and being chased by an almost naked Zulu warrior whose feet were even larger than those of the 'lady'. Another chap was clad in armour made from biscuit tins, complete with shield. Colonel A G Quilter came forward and said: 'We will now give the prizes; tomorrow we will give the Turks hell. By tomorrow I mean that in a few days' time we are going to land on the Gallipoli Peninsula. The eyes of the world will be upon us and the whole course of the war will depend on the success of our effort. We have to succeed and take Constantinople from the Turks. If we find it is impossible to land on the toe, we will try the neck, the Bulair Lines, or, failing there, at Enos.'

Now we knew officially where we were going. We had known unofficially before we left England; the whole world must have known.

Friday, April 16th

We entered Mudros harbour at 7 am as the *Royal George* and three transports were leaving. We turned about in the harbour and followed them. After a short while a destroyer came in very close. At once we turned about and headed for Lemnos. Rumour had it that a Turkish gunboat had been run ashore and destroyed by one of our destroyers.

After a while, we – like Dick Whittington – turned again and arrived at dusk in Trebuki Bay, Scyros. Instructions were posted at once for a dummy exercise. The Second Naval Brigade would be prepared to land on Turkish soil at 5 am (This was underlined in red crayon.) Everyone was extremely pleased that we were going to do something war-like at last.

Punctually at the appointed hour we climbed over the ship's side as we had done scores of times before and, with about forty in each boat, we rowed for the shore, soon to be joined by many other boats. In perfect formation we reached the rocky beach; we scrambled over the rocks and soon had a continuous line at the foot of the very steep slopes.

Immediately the order was given to take the hill. With short rushes we reached the summit after two hours and planted the Union Jack for all the world to see. Turkish soil – but we did not meet any Turks. We had added another small piece of land to the British Empire.

A prize was offered to the first section to reach the ship. Off we went at the double, over rocks and boulders, in and out of gullies, each section choosing their own particular route. Individuals and groups were to be seen everywhere but our section had managed to keep together and were satisfied that we stood a good chance of arriving first at the beach. Then it was reported to our Platoon Officer, Sub-Lieutenant Asquith[1], that someone had broken the shell of a large tortoise some distance back up the hill. He was furious and ordered us back to find it and put it out of its misery; we could not leave it there, suffering.

I wondered if, when the real fight began, should we kill those that were wounded so that they were not left behind to suffer?

Perhaps the rules of war, which I did not even pretend to know, allowed humans to suffer. People are inclined to turn a blind eye on individual suffering, especially if the suffering is out of sight. Maybe some day when war is brought to everyone's door-step then, and only then, will the peoples of the world wake up to the folly of mass slaughter as a means of settling international disputes.

My section lost the race but it had a new respect for its officer – a gentleman who, even on the eve of battle, had a soft heart and detestation of suffering.

We arrived at the water's edge to see the finish of a thrilling race to the ship. Lieutenant Freyberg just winning from Sub-Lieutenant Asquith after a powerful swim of no mean distance.

Friday, April 23rd

This was the original date for the landing on the Gallipoli Peninsula but on the 21st a strong wind sprang up and continued the whole day and the following night. Calm weather was essential for the landing of troops from open boats; each boat would have to make several journeys. In consequence, the landing was postponed for forty-eight hours. Although we did not realise

---

1 Son of the Prime Minister, Mr. H. H. Asquith. He was later made a brigadier, was seriously wounded and died at Clovelly in August 1939.

it at the time, this was an extension of life for many of the troops assembled in the area – a further two days to make our peace with our Maker. But for Sub-Lieutenant Rupert Brooke of 'A' Company, Hood Battalion, the sands had run out as he knew they would. He died of sunstroke and was buried in an olive grove on the island that evening. His poem The Soldier conveys his thoughts to the world in no uncertain manner:

> *If I should die, think only this of me;*
> *That there's some corner of a foreign field*
> *That is for ever England. There shall be*
> *In that rich earth a richer dust concealed;*
> *A dust whom England bore, shaped, made aware,*
> *A body of England's, breathing English air,*
> *Washed by the rivers, blest by suns of home.*

Saturday, April 24th

The transports in the harbour began to move. More than a hundred men from the Hood Battalion, with previous sea experience, had already left to serve as landing and beach parties. It was late evening when we steamed out of Trebuki Bay to the sound of cheering from the ships we passed. They were soon to follow us. Out of harbour, we were picked up by our escorting warships.

Sunday, April 25th

Just before dawn we appeared to have arrived at our rendezvous in the vicinity of Xeros Island at the north-east end of the gulf of that name. The ship's engines had considerably slowed and there was no visible wake. At sunrise two of the warships began bombarding the Peninsula while the fleet of transports lay in the background waiting to go in and land their troops. The warships continued to bombard the Bulair Line and this game of the cat watching the mouse continued all day.

We knew that there were troops on the shore; the Turks knew there were troops in the transports lying off-shore, waiting to land. The warships continued to lob their shells at the shore; we only stood and stared.

In the early afternoon. Leading Seaman Harris, my Section Leader, came and asked for volunteers who could swim – he had been ordered to get thirty men who were strong swimmers. I was the first of his section he met – volunteer number one. The remaining twenty-nine were soon lined up and taken below at once to the clothing store where we were issued with a new pair of canvas slippers, cardigan and a woollen cap-comforter. We then went to the armoury for two bandoliers containing fifty rounds each.

Afterwards came the briefing. We thirty men were going to be towed to withm 800 yards of the shore. From there, we would row ourselves the rest of the way. We were the bait and were to attract the enemy's attention so that they would be left in no doubt that this was the spot chosen for a landing. A fleet of transports had been in view all day so we could be sure of a warm reception.

The Australian and New Zealand forces had already gone ashore at Gaba Tepe a little farther down the coast and the 29th Division had landed at Cape Helles at the toe of the Peninsula. Our own little demonstration would force the Turkish Command to hold troops in readiness here-to contest a threatened landing. In the meantime, our troops already ashore would make good their footholds. They could also be reinforced.

At nine in the evening the 'suicide' party – as we were called – were given as much steaming hot cocoa as we could drink. Normally we did not get anything to eat or drink after tea. A wit referred to it as 'The Last Supper'.

At 10 pm we were ordered to man the ship's boat riding in the swell alongside. I led the way down Jacob's Ladder. We had been warned that there must be no talking and absolute silence must be maintained. I nipped down fairly quickly as I felt that if the chap following me stood on my fingers, I might forget the ban on talking.

When all were aboard we were eased off, the muffled oars slipped into the water and the suicide party was on its way. The oars cut the water as if they were handled by ghosts – not a sound, not a single light anywhere. Away from the shelter of our transport we felt very cold as we had left our tunics on board.

I was in the bow and Chief Petty Officer Milton was in the stern. I kept my eyes fixed straight ahead; it seemed a long way to the shore. More than half-an-hour after we had left the *Grantully Castle* a brilliant flash followed by a deafening noise broke the silence and revealed our position. A salvo from a warship a mile or so away, but the flash lit up the whole coastline, now looking very close.

I swung my rifle into firing position, felt for my bandoliers and prepared to jump. I had seen the cliffs a moment before but it was now darker than ever.

The bows struck something and swung away to starboard. It was so dark that there were times when I could not even see the sea. Were we lost? If it was the intention to land, why didnt we? If we were to attract attention only, why not a few rounds of rapid fire? We had rifles and a hundred rounds of ammunition each. It they were not to be used, why on earth did we bring them with us?

It was early in the morning when we came back on board the *Grantully Castle*. How we found the old ship I shall never know, but I was certainly very pleased. We had been out in an open boat for many hours and were so cold that it was difficult to climb up Jacob's Ladder. At once we were served with that beautiful piping hot cocoa – as much as we wanted.

During this time. Lieutenant Freyberg of 'A' Company had swum from the other ship's boat and lighted flares on the beach. He had to swim most of the way back to the ship before he was picked up.

Tuesday, April 27th

It appears that our demonstration has ended. We steamed down the coast to Gaba Tepe. The Australian and New Zealand forces did not appear to have advanced very far inland and we could see fighting taking place on the slopes running down to the beaches. There were many shell bursts on the hills beyond and more on the beach and in the sea. It was difficult to assess the position exactly from a distance but we could see the troops on the beach quite clearly as we steamed further down the coast.

We arrived off Cape Helles; at first glance the position here was much the same as at Gaba Tepe but as we moved round the Cape, things looked much better. Fighting was taking place all over the toe of the Peninsula; the fleet fired all day and we cruised round and round.

Wednesday, April 28th

We steamed up the coast again and once more took up a position off Gaba Tepe. The situation on shore looked much the same as yesterday; rifle fire and continuous shelling.

Thursday, April 29th

The Australians and the New Zealanders had advanced up the hillside; rifle fire and shelling had increased greatly. The warships were sending over salvo after salvo and we watched the shells bursting on the ridge.

Later in the afternoon we sailed away down the coast again to Cape Helles. There our troops had advanced during the hours of darkness.

During the night we landed on the Peninsula and took up positions on the slope above W beach. At daybreak the Turks began shelling us and kept it up all day. We went forward over the ridge and lay in support, digging funk holes in the long grass behind the firing line. There was a lot of sniping, the firing line was not a continuous line, just a series of outposts strung across the Peninsula.

Friday, April 30th

We moved into some derelict trenches captured during the advance of April 28th; this was the reverse line. The next morning we moved over to the left, still in support. Again we were in the open and throughout the day we moved about in groups, trying to find the snipers that were pestering us. We did not have much success; we probed the scrub and surrounded the small clumps of trees but the snipers still found their targets. The stray bullets added to our difficulties in defining me direction of the sniping.

Shortly after ten o'clock in the evening the Turks attacked. We moved quickly across to the right and took up a position across the Achi Baba Nullah, Anson Battalion going to the extreme right to assist the French, who were hard pressed.

CHAPTER SIX

MAY

Sunday, May 2nd

At dawn, groups of Turks were seen retiring, their attack having been repulsed. Hood and Howe Battalions moved over to the left. At ten o'clock on this beautiful Sunday morning, whilst the wild birds were singing merrily, we fixed bayonets and marched up the gully to attack, but the Turkish firing squad was waiting. We thought that, after the punishment we had given them during the night, they had moved out – but we were wrong. Machine-gun fire and shrapnel fire soon made us spread out as we continued to advance in short rushes for about four hundred yards. The machine-gun fire made further advance out of the question and we were ordered to dig in to obtain some shelter from the withering fire.

Our advance temporarily halted, the Second Hampshires came up to reinforce us, looking as though they were on parade. The Turks increased their shrapnel fire but the Hampshires came on in perfect formation even though the gaps in their line increased with every short rush. What was left of their brilliant regiment reached us in perfect formation. Their advance under such terrible fire was an object lesson to we civilian soldiers and the value of training was brought home to us during those glorious minutes. However, all our efforts were of no avail, so intense was the fire, and we were all ordered to retire to our original positions.

Later in the evening we got back to our bivouacs near 'W beach but this did not mean any rest. We worked like slaves digging holes to sleep in, but we never got a chance to use them: apart from fighting we had many other jobs to do; stores to be landed and rations to be carried. Men of all nationalities had to be buried where they fell or in a communal grave, to be trodden on by the living who came forward unaware of what the soil beneath their feet was hiding.

Monday, May 3rd

Still in support as we were the only men available – none but us between the front line and the sea. If the Turks break through on any part of the line, the whole front must collapse. The Twenty-Ninth Division was very solid, fighting without a moment's pause. The Senegalese-French troops on the right flank are not at all solid. Late last night the French again fell back. Anson Battalion went over to the right to stop the rot.

The Senegalese troops seemed to be afraid of the dark. They put up rapid fire in all directions and then decided to retire. We seem to have the permanent job of retaking the trenches the Senegalese vacate, yet whilst we are with them they are excellent fighters. Their broad, everlasting grins soon captivate even the most dour of us.

Tuesday, May 4th

We appear to have got quite a few guns ashore; they and the French quick-firing '75s' plastered the Turks who heartily reciprocated.

Just before dawn, heavy firing broke out on the extreme left. The French on the right joined in and soon the whole line from the Straits to the sea was in turmoil but it died down shortly after daybreak. With the exception of sporadic outbursts, the line was comparatively quiet but the warships off-shore were doing a bit of shelling. We, however, are at peace but it is too noisy to sleep even though we are all desperately tired but it's nice to know the ships are still there. Although we cannot see them firing, we can. see their shells bursting on the slopes of Achi Baba. It must be uncomfortable up there for the Turks.

At six in the evening we took over from the French the trenches across the Achi Baba Nulla (later known as Back-house Post as it was hereabouts that the GOC, Second Naval Brigade, Commodore Backhouse, established his Headquarters). In fact we had returned to where we were on the night of April 30th.

The line at this point consisted of a series of funk-holes, each about two feet deep. The French had stuck bayonets into the ground and stretched a wire across the road up the nullah. To this wire they had tied a number of old jam tins with stones inside them; not by any standards effective but the idea was there. The wire was smooth and pulled out in concertina fashion; much more use could have been made of it had it been better positioned.

The sector was quiet and we sat under the stunted trees and among the bushes and brewed tea. The Turks were miles away – or so it seemed – but snipers were active. A strange feeling to be sitting at ease in the front line, without a care. The French had retired from this very spot on two occasions recently-but it was quiet now. At last we have our own sector, a welcome change to all that chasing from one side of the Peninsula to the other.

As usual, when it began to get dark the French on our right commenced their rapid fire. They must have fired in all directions again as two of us were wounded by their long copper bullets. The firing spread along the entire front.

Thursday, May 6th

After a fairly quiet night we were told at daybreak that we were to advance this morning in support of the French. We are not too happy; still, their Colonial troops seem fine when we are with them. You cannot help liking them even if they do get panicky in the dark.

Later on in the morning we were told that the orders had been changed. We were still to be under the command of the French General d'Amade, but were to advance in conjunction with them and not in support. We were to be the left flank of the French line. Hood Battalion leading and Howe Battalion in support. The whole line would advance at eleven o'clock with the village of Krithia as the first objective. The French are to move along the Kereves Dere ridge on the right flank and the Naval Division will advance in the centre, keeping in touch with both flanks. The second objective is for the Twenty-ninth Division to capture the two hills north-west of Krithia, thus making the village untenable. The third objective would be Achi Baba itself.

At eleven o'clock we moved up the Achi Baba Nullah in Indian file until we were in open country and then spread out, advancing in short rushes. Immediately in front of us was a swamp which we were ordered to cross. The Turkish fire was murderous and we lost a lot of men. There were no trenches to be seen but the Turks must have had their machine-guns perfecfly sighted. It was terrifying; fewer men rose after each rush – but we still charged forward blindly, repeatedly changing direction, but it did not appear to make the slightest difference. The fire was coming from all directions yet we could not see a single Turk or any sign of a trench.

We appeared to be making for a white house and rushed through a small vineyard to capture it. We then took up a position along a small ridge just beyond the house where we were joined by several small groups. We counted ourselves; in all there were about fifty of us, including Horton, Townsend, Yates and myself.

We had to alter direction by swinging round to take up a new position behind a second small ridge at right angles to the first. There was a gateway about twenty yards to my right, which looked like the entrance to the vineyard. We were ordered to go through and spread out beyond. There must have been a machine-gun trained on this opening. We had to climb over the dead and dying and then run about thirty yards before falling down in a patch of prickly scrub. After a little while I heard Townsend calling to me and, without raising my head, I crawled towards him. Horton and Yates were somewhere behind and crawled up later. There was no one else moving; we were the only ones to get through that opening.

We decided that there appeared to be better cover in the thicker scrub about ten yards ahead of us. We ran forward and, as we reached it, Yates was hit below the abdomen. He bent to his knees, rolled over and then got to his feet again, turning round and round. He rushed forward but fell groaning after a few yards. The three of us crawled forward towards him. Horton reached him first but while trying to comfort him was shot through the head. The same bullet, spent though it was, took a piece out of my knuckle. Poor Horton died crying for his mother; he always maintained he was eighteen but he certainly didn't look more than sixteen at the very most. He was a great fellow; in civil life he was a steward on a banana boat. Totally unsuited for this rough life, he never once complained. Always willing and eager to help, he himself was now beyond help. There was nothing Townsend or I could do for him or for Yates.

No one else came forward. The bullets were hitting the sandy soil all round us, the dust getting in our eyes – how soon would it be before they hit us? Townsend suggested that we should move forward. It took courage to rise but nowhere could be worse than here. Together we ran forward with the bullets singing in the air and pitting the ground. Ten to fifteen yards' run and we buried our heads in that prickly, beastly smelling scrub but there was no respite.

It must have been two hours since we began our advance. There was not a soul in sight, friend or foe, neither had we seen one single trench. If only we knew where everybody was; if only we knew where anyone was. We kept moving carefully but with no particular object in view, save trying to avoid the hail of lead that seemed to be following us. Obviously our movements were being watched by the Turks, but where the devil were they?

There was a small mound some distance to the right. After many short rushes we reached it and for the first time since we started we felt comparatively safe. We took stock of our position; we had not yet fired a single round. It we could only get a glimpse of a single Turk we would have some idea of the direction we should take. We rested for a while and came to the conclusion that we had advanced too far and that our best course would be to dig ourselves in and wait. I was anxious to get more cover but the constant fire scared me stiff. Townsend sat up and with his entrenching tool commenced to dig. This movement brought even more lead towards us. We lay flat again – the bullets were coming from all directions. Townsend said he thought we were surrounded; I had thought so long ago!

Over to the right about a hundred yards away we could see what appeared to be a ditch. We could not stay where we were much longer, so, with a dash of about thirty yards to begin with, we set off in that direction. A few more shorter rushes brought us close enough to crawl the last ten or so yards into the ditch, which was barely eighteen inches deep. We felt much safer now. We had only guessed its existence because of the long green grass. There was a little water here and there, rather stagnant of course, but it quenched our thirsts. We chewed the grass, which reminded me of my father saying that we should all have to eat grass before the war was over.

What a stroke of luck to find this tiny oasis. It was easy to dig here and the rain of lead seemed to be high overhead now. We recommenced digging and soon had quite a small but comfortable hole. A little water trickled in but water anywhere or of any sort was an asset out here. Now that we had a fort we arranged for one of us to rest whilst the other kept a look-out. Sitting in the water, I fell asleep, for how long I don't know, Donald – that was Townsend's Christian name – awakened me saying he thought he could see someone moving on the left near a solitary tree which we had been near a little while ago. For a second I saw three moving figures, then they were gone. We agreed that if our sense of direction was correct, they should be our men. True, we had been fired on from that angle most of the afternoon but then we had been fired on from all angles. We decided to keep a sharp eye out for them in any case.

We were conscious of the fact that our faces were burnt almost black and that we had not washed for a week. Our sun helmets we discarded days ago as the extended piece at the back was all right for protecting the necks whilst we were standing but when we lay flat they would fall off as we raised our heads to fire! We were wearing woollen cap comforters only and could easily be taken for Turks whose headgear was similar. At the moment this was not so good.

If the figures beside that tree would only move again we would be pleased, but war is most unobliging sometimes. I promised Don that I would keep my eye on the tree if he would rest a while and he was soon asleep. I kept my eyes glued in that direction for quite a while but on glancing round to look at Don I saw the French Senegalese coming up a long way behind and on our right, but coming in our direction. I gave Don a gentle kick. In a flash he was levelling his rifle at them but pulled himself together, apologising. 'I thought it was Johnnie,' he said. What about the other side? They must be Turks after all.

For the first time since we began to advance we knew our position – and what a lousy position it was! We were in between the advancing French and the Turin. Right bang in the middle and both sides were firing in our direction. To make matters worse, it was getting dark. We hoped that these big black fallows would reach us before it was really dark as it would confuse matters if they didn't.

We were keeping low and discussing how we could attract their attention when Don spotted at least a dozen Turks beside that tree and opened fire. We were having a bit of our own back now. It was like shooting rabbits – waiting for them to run, then Bang!

We had been the rabbits all day; now we were the game-keepers, and about time too. We had a few moments ago been wondering how we could attract attention but now our firing solved that. The Senegalese began to pay us far too much attention for our liking – it was bad for our health. Of course they were not to know that we two were on their side and that hours ago we had captured the ground they were now trying to gain.

Where the devil had they been all this while anyway? However, this was not the time nor place to argue and, judging by their fire, they were in no mood for argument The light was fading but we could see them quite plainly. We stuck our woollen caps on our bayonets and waved cautiously but this made things worse. We were certainly in a bit of a jam. It looked certain we should be shot if we stood up but if we laid low until they reached us they would stick us like pigs and I didn't care much for their very long three-cornered bayonets. They, like us, had suffered much from snipers so we couldn't expect any mercy. We would have to sort this lot out and sharply as they were less than fifty yards away. One more rush and they would be upon us.

As we had good cover we agreed to lie low until they were almost upon us, then jump up and hope that it worked. Mercifully for Don and me they just kept firing, taking no aim whatsoever but simply letting off their rifles. We jumped up but our timing was a fraction too soon and we had to parry their thrust, calling out 'Ingleesh Johnnie, Ingleesh'. I could have run my man through quite easily but instead I swung my butt round, catching him square on the jaw with such force that he sank to the ground. At once I tried to pick him up but another six-footer rushed towards me. I met him with a parry but he came with such a force that neither of us could rectify our moves. We collided so violently that we were both partially winded and each of us lost our rifles. We were having a real rough-house when my monster was wounded in the leg and thank goodness for that. He could not get up and I kept repeating 'Ingleesh, Ingleesh Johnnie'.

What a relief when I saw that infectious grin on his ebony face. Don was having a rare go with three burly fellows. He had one on the ground when my wounded former opponent cried out something I did not understand. It gave Don a breather but they kept him covered. They could shoot him now, but Don didn't seem to realise this. He just stood laughing and when he made a move towards me one of his opponents fired but missed.

My wounded chap called out again sharply and the broad grins spread all round. We were accepted as brothers.

It suddenly dawned on us that we were standing in the open; we soon altered that as we lay waiting for the order to advance I took a piece of rag from the pocket of the wounded Senegalese and tied it round his leg. He had got over the shock and we were friends now. When the order came to advance be came limping forward with us. My first opponent was now sitting up but he looked so vague that we left him there to finish his dream.

It was nearly dark now and we two once white-faced men amongst a crowd of blacks advanced up the slight slope and dug in. The advance was at an end for the day and I had not yet seen the Turkish trenches.

I did not know what was happening on the other parts of the line. We appeared to be ahead but according to the brieflng we received before starting this morning, we should be somewhere near the top of Achi Baba. We must be at least a mile nearer to the summit and yet we had not captured one single trench today. The flanks were well behind. When we started off we were in the centre, but the opposition at the white bouse had apparently caused us to ease to the left and we may have lost touch with the French on our right. After we had overrun the house we were attempting to get back to the right when the machine-gun fire wiped out the lot, with the exception of Don and me. That would have been at about one o'clock in the afternoon.

It was quite dark now; the French had just come up, but we had been here for hours. There must still be a gap between us and the rest of the Naval chaps. During the night Don and I made our way to the extreme left and found there was quite a big gap but there were plenty of Senegalese to fill it. We managed to close it and join up with a party of the Howe Battalion and were soon all fairly well dug in and settled down to await the next move. There were not many Howes but we could now talk to someone with a common language instead of having to use our hands.

Friday, May 7th

Just before dawn every other man was ordered to keep a sharp look-out over the parados and to fire on sight. There appeared to be as many Turks behind our line as there were in front. We were kept very busy for quite a while but by sunrise we had things under control and we settled down again to our normal way of trench life – one hour on watch, one hour off – when you do anything and everything there is to be done, including sleeping if you can, eating and drinking if you have anything to eat or drink. We tidied up our ditch; it is not a trench although we have been digging all night but it does afford us some cover. I don't suppose we shall stay here long; we never do stay long anywhere and we have an appointment in Constantinople for which we are already late. It was a lovely day and the sun was strong.

At about noon the Turks attacked in force. They were all over the place – hundreds of them – and they all seemed to be in a hurry. Maybe they had an appointment with someone on one of the beaches. What a change from yesterday. It was really encouraging to see some of those blighters who had led Don and me such a dance all day. Quite a lot of them won't do so again. We could not miss – not that we wanted to. It was incredible that men could still come forward but they did, and some came so near they fell into our ditch, their fighting days over. They just added to the many that already lay around but their courage will live long in my mind.

All around me, very excited Senegalese fired their rifles as fast as they could, not caring much where their bullets went. They had no idea of taking aim; if they happened to be facing the rear then that was the direction of their fire. It was just bad luck for the Turk if our black friend happened to be facing his way. There were only a handful of naval men taking aim and doing any real damage but we were happy the Senegalese were still with us. If only they would cool down and take aim, we could soon smash this attack. We had reasonable cover; the Turks were in the open but they still came forward. Some crawled through the burning scrub in front of us and managed to reach our line but were promptly dealt with. Whether it was the burning scrub or our rifle fire I don't know but there were not so many targets now. Another attack had failed; we could see small groups retiring and we helped them on their way, leaving the burning scrub to consume those who were not already dead.

The sun was still high in the heavens; the air stifling and the stench nauseating. Both Don and I were starving but we had neither food nor water. Our black friends, though, had plenty and readily shared it with us. God bless them! We quaffed their red wine and enjoyed it; it was good to be alive.

Except for sporadic firing, our part of the line was quiet. Our units on the extreme left appeared to be engaged in heavy fighting. As we were now about a mile ahead of them, we asked some Howe chap where to find our own battalion. They said that the Hood Battalion should be in the support line. They could not say for sure though as, in an attempt to maintain contact with the French, they, like Don and I, had got mixed up with them and when trying to reach their own crowd they had isolated themselves. They were in line but not in touch.

More blacks came up and, as this was their sector, we whites moved to the left in search of the rest of our own crowd and met up with the Ansons. They confirmed that the Hoods were in support. They had not been attacked this morning but knew that we had. We were excused look-out duties because of this. Don and I didn't need any rocking. I fell off to sleep as soon as I sat down. How long I slept I have not the faintest idea. I was awakened by Don kicking my shins. I wondered it he ever slept and asked him so.

'On your hind legs. Stand by to attack.'

What, again? Are we fighting this war on our own?

Come on, you said you could do it,' and, with a fatherly pull, I was on my feet and wide awake.

It appears that the left had failed in their advance yesterday and again today. To relieve the pressure on the left, the centre and the French on the right must attack.

Just before five in the evening we set off to make contact with the main Turkish army; we just had to defeat it and then walk at ease to Constantinople. Well, that's what they told us. We had been playing with the enemy up to now.

We went forward a few hundred yards. It was slow and heavy going up a slight slope and about sunset we were ordered to dig in. We were a long way ahead of the flanks, both of which had been held up yet again. The French on the right, however, had made some progress up the face of the Kereves Dere ridge.

So another day draws to a close. With the setting of the sun the majority of sane people prepare for the coming night and a peaceful rest. We prepared for a nightmare. We knew we should be counter-attacked and everyone must be watchful. All through the night we were subjected to intense fire. The routine of one hour on and one off went by the board – it was almost continuous look-out. If not on watch you dared not close your eyes. If you did it meant being instantly awakened to fire to kill or remove someone who had been killed. It is surprising the effect dead men have upon you. Whilst a fight is in progress I seem not to notice anyone, dead or alive. I have only the desire for self-preservation. There are times when an uneasy feeling compels me to move, maybe only a foot so, and then feel perfectly safe. Most of us are the same. Some know they are going to die – some even know when. They come and shake you by the hand and bid you 'Goodbye'. Strangely enough they do not appear to be afraid.

War is a queer pastime! it plays havoc with all reasoning. What is essential one minute is of no importance the next. You carry things around with you that you think you cannot do without, yet when you lose them you wonder why on earth you burdened yourself with so much rubbish. You make pals and lose them. You make more pals and lose them too. You long for the daylight and yet when the sun rises, bringing with it both light and warmth, you long for the darkness and the cool refreshing air.

There is a feeling of security in the hours that are distant, – the hours that never come. The present is hell and the morrow – what will it bring? New tortures or new hope? Perhaps it will bring both.

Saturday, May 8th

As the sun rose over the hill we rejoiced at its coming. In peace it brings life; in war it brings death, but it also brings hope. We cherished that hope, yet in our own minds we knew that before this same sun went down beyond the blue sea behind us, many that now rejoiced and hoped would be rotting beneath its burning rays. Some of them would die without a murmur, others struggle for hours, but death would win in the end. There is nothing one can do save hope and pray. In war you kill and expect to be killed. Every now and then you realise you are still alive and thank God and wonder.

Way over on the left fighting had begun again. Our men were attacking. After a while we were told what we already knew – our attack had failed. Many would be left to die of their wounds or of thirst, tormented by millions of flies. A few yards of scrub-covered ground had been wrested from the enemy but not enough. We must attack again to ease the pressure and prevent the Turks from counter-attacking. We must force them to keep their reserves opposing us. Our guns opened up on the whole front, a short but heavy bombardment.

At about the same time as yesterday (five o'clock in the evening) another general advance was in full swing. We went forward on the extreme left of the French and made good progress. For a while we were in touch with them but before nightfall there was a gap between us. I don't know whether we had veered to the left or they to the right Maybe it was the machine-gun fire that was responsible for the gap. Our little force, comprising two Hoods, about a dozen Howes and – at a guess – about thirty Ansons, kept in line with the French and was later joined by fewer than a score of our black friends. But the gap still remained until more Hoods and Howes came up to close it

We were on top of a small ridge. The French had made their way further along the Kereves Dere ridge and appeared to have gone some way up the face. On our left the Australians had also made substantial headway but they were not quite in line with us although they had advanced further than we had today. The line still bent back towards the sea.

At about eight in the evening the order was passed along the line for everyone to move towards the left as quickly as possible. There was yet another gap – on the left this time – between us and the Australians. The Turks were breaking through in force.

With open warfare these gaps must occur unless you have plenty of reserves. We did not appear to have any reserves at all, – hence the gaps. The Australian and New Zealand Brigade had been brought from Gaba Tepe to help us out and were all engaged today. The New Zealanders were with the Twenty-ninth Division on the left flank and the Australians with the Royal Naval Division in the centre. In support to us were the Drake Battalion and the Plymouth Marines. It was the Drakes that halted the breakthrough.

The Marines came up in the early hours of the morning and finally closed the gap. When the fighting died down we were ordered back to our own battalions but the question was, where were they?

Sunday, May 9th

The Drake Battalion had taken over this part of the line. A very young-looking officer of the Howe Battalion collected his remaimng six men and, with the two Hoods (Don and me), we all started on the way back. It was almost as difficult to get back as it was to go forward. One has a different feeling when you have your back to the oncoming bullets. You feel you ought to turn round to face the music, but one cannot walk backwards here – it is difficult enough to walk forwards.

When we were clear of the line we rested for a little while until daybreak before making our way across the open country. It was almost noon when we finally found the Hoods. They had been relieved last night and were now in reserve, grouped amongst a clump of bushes with the occasional tree here and there.

We had apparently been given up as lost and were greeted by a certain Chief Petty-Officer (I won't mention his name) with a remark that inferred that we had successfully dodged the column. Happily it was heard by the Howe officer who promptly halted us and made us face him. He then told the CPO just what he thought of him. Such a dressing-down in front of the ranks staggered us. The CPO apologised to the officer and then to us – a most unusual thing to do, but the act of a gentleman; we admired him for this.

Now we had found comparative safety, Don went scrounging for biscuits whilst I went in search of water. I made my way to a nearby ditch – full of hope until I reached it. Not a drop of water anywhere. I dug a hole and waited but still no water. My throat was parched so, with a stone in my mouth, I returned to find Don had managed to get hold of a couple of biscuits. I swear these biscuits were even harder than the stone I was sucking and probably almost as old. We had one biscuit each and a stone to suck and enjoyed both.

Later we were lined up for a roll call. In my own company, 'C', there were present only three officers, ninety NCO's and men. These figures were given to me by the CPO, whilst enquiring from Don and me if we had knowledge of any other men whom we may have seen whilst we were with the French during the last few days. We had not seen any. Of course, there may have been many more knocking about who might turn up later. I knew of many who would not; we had lost at least half our strength in nine days' fighting. The Hood – Battalion Commander, Lieutenant-Colonel Quilter, was killed early on May 6th. He went forward carrying an oversized walking stick.

Monday, May 10th

The Turks attacked the French and the Naval battalions on the left of the French. We were immediately behind them in reserve, but were not called upon to go forward. We stood by in readiness all the morning.

Thursday, May 13th

We were relieved from the supports by the Manchesters of the 42nd Division. They had landed from Egypt on the evening of the sixth. It would have helped considerably if they had been available for the attack on that day or the subsequent attacks the following days. They seemed a nice lot of chaps.

We moved into an orchard on top of a small plateau some considerable distance from the front line. This was to be our rest camp when not in the forward positions. We were in full view of the Turks, of course; we had not yet captured enough ground to be otherwise. Trees were few and far between and afforded practically no screen and very little shade. Each man collected either a pick or a shovel and began bis own grave-like hole, roughly six feet long and two feet wide. There was about a foot of soil and then broken rocks. The general depth would be about two feet. Our waterproof sheets, held in position over the top by pieces of rock, completed our abode when and if we got the opportunity to occupy them. A few shells from the slopes off Achi Baba helped us to find that extra energy to get some cover quickly. There was a much bigger shell coming from the Asiatic side but so far as we were concerned, it was falling short, somewhere in the lower ground to the right They would have to increase their range to reach this much higher ground. At night we could see the flash as it was fired. The shell burst and then we heard the noise it made during its flight across the Straits. We called her Asiatic Annie'.

De Tott's French battery and the Navy hurled hundreds of shells at her, but she continued firing.

Friday, May 14th

We were inspected by General d'Amade on the rising ground that led to our camp. We had been under his command since May 6th and he was now returning us to our General, Sir Archibald Paris, somewhat more than slightly worn. We presented the distinguished general with a machine-gun we had captured in the white house on May 6th. In his short speech of thanks he spoke of the fine qualities, the devotion to duty, the courage and intrepidity of we three battalions under his command during May 6th, 7th, 8th and 9th.

'Every French soldier who has seen you work renders homage' – now, wasn't that nice. To lose more than half your pals, many lying disembowelled a few hundred yards away; those who had so far escaped, half famished, skulking in holes, waiting to fight again, had to listen to this international courtesy.

Every French soldier renders homage. My answer would be brief: 'This is no good when having to write home telling a mother or a wife how my pal, their son or husband, had died bravely.' We did not have much time to write letters. It's a rotten business, anyway, telling our relatives to call round to a neighbour with the tragic news or with words of comfort if she knows already. Perhaps the poor soul finds comfort in these kind words. I know, too, that maybe tomorrow or even, tonight someone will be writing to my home. Who knows, who cares! Life is very cheap out here. There is nothing you can do except keep your head down and your heart up.

Tuesday, May 18th

We have been on working parties for the last three days, sometimes up to the reserve lines and sometimes working on 'W' beach, which was just as well. Our rest camp had been shelled very heavily in our absence and we had quite a bit of tidying up to do when we returned each night but today we stayed at home. Only an occasional shell came our way.

After tea the company were detailed for working parties, to leave at eight o'clock. We never know where we are going or what we have to do until we arrive on the job, not that it makes any difference but there was a difference tonight. My platoon had not been detailed to do anything. It was the first time we had missed work but we did not raise any objections. We made ourselves scarce by remaining in our funk-holes, expecting to be hauled out at any moment It was near enough eight o'clock and the working-party was parading in readiness to move off. They were some little distance away from us, over to the right, when a salvo of shrapnel burst very low over the camp, scattering the parade. Luckily there were only a few casualties among them but in our platoon there were many, even though we were in our funk-holes which were not deep enough to afford much cover in such circumstances. The shrapnel burst over our heads.

The working party was cancelled but not because of this. It was apparently cancelled before the shelling because within a quarter of an hour we – at least all those able to walk – were on our way to the firing line. It was a rotten journey, stopping and starting, turning back, then going forward again. I suppose the leading men took the wrong ditch where it forked or went too far before turning left or right. It happens all the time – any journey to the line is extremely arduous, especially if you are on the tail end of a long file.

Reaching the support line we collected either a pick or a shovel and continued towards the firing line. We didn't bother to stop there but went forward into the unknown for about four hundred yards. I hoped the officer who was leading knew where he was going. In the darkness we spread out into some sort of a line and dug in. There were a lot of bodies lying about but we only moved those that were in the way.

By dawn we had a good, almost continuous trench about three feet deep, roughly three to four hundred yards ahead of our original firing line. In my little sphere only two men had been wounded by stray bullets; there were plenty flying about all night but they were high overhead. The nearer we were to the Turks, the safer we seemed to be – at least that was how it had been tonight.

About an hour before dawn all work ceased and we 'Stood to' as was usual at this time of the day. This meant that everyone was on look-out After dawn, sentries were posted, ration parties detailed and the rest of us set to making the trench ship-shape – a little deeper here or raising the parapet there. There were all sorts of local jobs that had to be done – with your head well down of course. A sudden burst of machine-gun fire reminded us that Old Man Turk was still about though we could not see any sort of trench. He was very cleverly concealed in the broken ground and scrub somewhere out there in front. He is a wily old devil but did not worry us unduly until a ration party set off. No sooner were they clear of the trench when he opened up with his machine-guns – not a long burst but, long enough to wipe out the party. Those that were wounded would have to stay there all day in the blazing sun as every movement brought another burst of fire. We answered back in an attempt to keep him quiet whilst another party set off but they too were shot down long before they reached that stretch of low lying ground about a hundred yards behind us.

A third party set off from a different part of the line, a sloping trench having been cut so that the men could get out of the trench by crawling, but that was the last we saw of them.

We were not so much hungry as thirsty; we had not brought anything with us because of the digging we had to do. We began to make a communication trench out of the sloping cut that had been made to let the ration party out. Only one man could work at a time. It was slow and dangerous to begin with as each shovelful of earth thrown out was met by a bullet. Three men were shot in the head; they must have shown their heads as they threw the earth out My mining experience came in useful; I could throw the earth in any direction from a stooping position. You have to keep your head down in the mines as well as in war.

The chap I relieved had purposely turned a little to the right I turned slightly left so that when the trench was completed it would be zig-zag, which would prevent direct fire down it

Whilst in the firing line, in between spells of digging, we were heartened to see a scattered group of men making for our line – short rush, then a considerable crawl, another rush and another crawl. They were a long way from us but each rush brought those that were able just that little bit nearer. Each individual acted on his own Initiative and decided the length of his rush. On they came and up went our hopes. Each time they lay down to bury their beads in the prickly scrub our hopes went down with them but they still came on – at least some of them did.

I was detailed to do a bit more digging. It was now late afternoon and we had a long way to go but we were satisfied with our progress. The rifle fire seemed to have ceased. We were working in pairs now and had turned to the left again. It was much better like this with someone to help and to talk to. My mate was digging and I used the shovel. He said he saw someone in the open; I had a very cautious peep but couldn't see anyone so continued with the digging.

Again my mate said he could see someone and pointed out where but I still couldn't see anyone. We both had a peep together and as he was pointing out the direction to me, we saw him, a one-man ration party, get to his feet, pick up what looked like a dixie and move hurriedly forward; he did not run.

We, in unison, called to him to come towards us. I am certain he heard our call as he looked directly at us. It would have meant his moving almost directly left, but he had set out to go forward and forward he must go. Dazed though he was, forward was his only direction. He lay down for a minute or two and then struggled to his feet, picking up his perforated dixie. With determination and defiance on his face he slowly walked the remaining ten yards to our trench, unmolested. The Turks must have seen him as it was daylight. He was assisted into the trench, still holding his dixie with about a cupful of tea in it He was in a terrible mess; how he managed to walk at all I shall never understand. His right thigh muscle appeared to be completely shot away and he had two more bullets in his right arm. Goodness knows how many more he had in his body. Our thirst was made more acute by the sight of that cupful of cold tea but no man would dream of touching it whilst there was the least sign of life in the chap who had brought it. As he lay exhausted, almost unconscious, there was always someone in attendance, dipping a finger in the precious liquid and wetting the poor chap's lips. We sucked stones and moistened our own lips with urine, which made them smart but it was moisture and that was all that mattered at the moment.

How pleased we all were when the sun sank down behind us. The, shallow trench now protected us not only from the Turks but from the setting sun. At this time of the evening the sun shone in the Turk's face and apparently because of this he kept his firing up until the sun sank beyond the sea. Usually as the light faded, so did the firing, but tonight he kept it up; he even increased it. We dismissed all thought of relief while this was going on as our reliefs would have to come up in the open and would have no hope of reaching us.

Just about midnight the Turk began to attack, not in the usual manner but in small isolated groups, some of which managed to get near our line. None succeeded in reaching it, though, but they kept coming for over an hour. We expected they would come in force any minute but, as time passed, the whok line gradually quietened down. In the meantime, whilst the attack was in progress, one of our men stood by our now unconscious tea-carrier, ready to shoot him it we were forced to retire, rather than leave him to the Turks.

In the early hours of the morning we were relieved. The reliefs had been waiting for hours for the firing to ease and had suffered quite a lot as they were for the most part between the two trenches.

We knew that it would soon be daylight and as the communication trench was by no means finished it would mean that our wounded friend would have to wait until it was before he could be taken back. We took him with us, two at his head and two at his feet, the carrying-party leading the way. When I we changed over, the rest of the batch waited until the bearers were on their way again before moving off. Four hundred yards is not a long way but it seemed so before we finally reached the trench and handed him to the stretcher-bearers. I had no further news of this gallant gentleman; I hope he survived his ordeal. With such courage as he had I feel sure he refused to die. I have many times seen his image and benefited from his determination and courage and his will to accomplish his task stands out in my mind.

Thursday, May 20th

After thirty-three hours without food or water we were back in our so-called trench, much deeper now than when we previously passed through it. The former occupants had converted the series of hastily dug funk-holes into quite a nice trench and we were improving on their work. We could now move about in safety and comfort; it is nice to be able to stretch your legs once in a while. It appears that our tactics of advancing and digging in and then moving forward again, groping for the Turk's positions and losing quite a lot of men in doing so, does not achieve the desired result We seem to be committed to trench warfare and all our ideas of capturing Achi Baba in a single day would have to be forgotten for the time being. Each day while we wait for reinforcements that never come, the Turk is getting his. The arrival of the Forty-second at the beginning of the month did not even make up for our losses. If only we had a couple of those divisions that were sight-seeing in Egypt!

Friday, May 21st

We were relieved from the support line late in the evening and made our-way back to our rest camp. It amuses me to write 'rest camp'. Working all night in the front lines or on one of the beaches and being shelled in camp all day. But today we had some splendid news via the Peninsula Press, a single sheet of paper posted on a tree. It said that a force of 20,000 fresh troops from Constantinople attacked the Australian lines on the 19th but were repulsed, leaving over 2,000 dead. If they left that many dead there must have been another 3,000 lying wounded in the open. Many of them would die in the blazing sun. The Australian and New Zealand foothold is about a mile and a half wide, with both flanks resting on the sea. The furthermost part of the arc is about a thousand yards inland. It was Liman von Sanders's intention to drive them into the sea. Now that he has failed we can expect him to have a go at us here at Cape Helles. His fresh troops won't have to be very fresh to be in a fitter condition than we. For over three weeks we have attacked and been counter-attacked. The shortage of food and water, the blazing sun, the stench from the rotting corpses everywhere and the millions of flies has sapped most of the life out of us. Why were the dead not buried? Easier said than done. Show your head for one second and you are on the list for burial. Day or night, anything that moves is fired on. Of course we managed to bury some but the majority are out of reach. Within a matter of hours corpses that are exposed to the sun swell to an incredible size. Whatever nationality, they remain where they fall until we advance through them on our way forward to that distant hill that appears to be mocking us.

By the sound of things on the extreme right the French are trying to pinch a bit more of that Kereves Dere ridge that runs diagonally to our front. This ridge commands not only the French sector but also that of the Naval Division. Any advance on our front alone could not be maintained if the Turks remained in possession of the ridge. Later on during the evening we were told that the French had made considerable progress. Good for them. I hope they hold on to their gains.

Whit Sunday, May 23rd

We are still 'resting', unloading lighters off 'W' beach, each of us carrying a box from the lighter to the beach and returning with a lump of rock in an effort to maintain the pier. The sea as well as the Turks seem to resent our being here. We have dumped tons of rock in between the iron stakes that define the pier, for the angry sea to gobble up.

We were quite suddenly hurriedly assembled on the beach and marched off towards the firing line. We moved about until dawn. Goodness knows where we had been; there couldn't be many places where we had not been! Although we did not go into the front line trench, we were much too near to be comfortable on many occasions. The units of the Naval Division that had been with the Australians at Gaba Tepe had by now joined the rest of the Division at Cape Helles. We had our own section of the line and each battalion occupying the front trench had its own idea of improving it It was one of these improvements that was going on tonight They had gone forward a few hundred yards during the darkness, without serious losses, and dug another trench. Much the same operation as ours on the night of the eighteenth and, I believe, equally successful.

Whit Monday, May 24th

It was midday when we arrived back in our rest camp. Like all willing horses we soon found ourselves on the way back to 'W' beach as a working party. We were told that we would be required in an hour which could only mean one thing. So we had one hour in the cool sea – after all, it is holiday time. Asiatic Annie dropped a single shell amongst us – one dead and five wounded – but the work and the bathing went on uninterrupted. So did the shelling. The French battery on the point at the entrance to the Straits sent over a few in return but Asiatic Annie was not impressed; she would pack up when she was ready.

You may have noticed by now I have made little mention of food. We live on what is known as 'hard tack'. Cast iron biscuits and water when you can get either. Once a day, if you are lucky, there is bully beef and fly stew as the main meal. For breakfast you might get a rasher of salty bacon and a mug of fly tea. I am sure they boil the bacon in the tea. In the evening we have another mug of fly tea and either a piece of slimy, fly-covered cheese or share a small tin of apricot jam between the lot of us. As one opens the tin the flies are so thick that they are squashed in the process. One never sees the jam; one can only see a blue-black mixture of sticky, sickly flies. They drink the sweat on our bodies and our lips and eyes are always covered with them. As we wipe them away we squash them, thereby making more moisture for the others that take their place. There is no escape from them. The hundreds we eat do not seem to lessen the swarm. They are forever present, night and day.

Friday, May 28th

Unlucky Friday they say. Well, so far it has been by no means unlucky for us. We arrived on 'W' beach before breakfast. Again we were told we could have an hour in the water before commencing work. This is a nice habit we are getting into. For a whole hour we knew exactly what we had to do. We were ordered to parade under the cliffs at 7.30 and see that we were all there on time. We lost no time in getting into the water. It was cool and refreshing.

About a dozen of us swam towards HMS *Majestic* lying close inshore. All the other warships and transports had gone. My intention was to get near enough to scrounge something to eat. The lads afloat had plenty to spare and a stale loaf would be improved by a dip in the sea. I have not seen any bread since coming ashore over a month ago but I think I would recognise a loaf if one is aimed at me.

I was deluding myself that I would reach the ship first. I had about a five-yard lead and was swimming strongly when I heard a deep thud and the water seemed to vibrate violently. I got a lovely mouthful and, half choked, struck out frantically. I thought I had struck the wash from a trawler. I had lost sight of the *Majestic* and no wonder, for I had been turned completely round and was swimming away from her. Puzzled for the moment, I suddenly realised that she was heeling over. Her torpedo nets were out and hundreds of men were lining her deck. Many dived, some jumped and others scrambled over on to her side as she slowly heeled over. How amazingly cool everyone seemed to be. Those that jumped took their time; they ambled to a suitable spot and took the plunge, quite unconcernedly so it seemed. In a matter of minutes only the keel was showing above the water like a huge whale. The only visible sign of any urgency was a solitary figure, carrying what appeared to be a small bundle, hurrying along the keel to avoid getting his feet wet as the stern became awash. The bow of the keel remained above the water and there sat the solitary sailor on his bundle.

The old but faithful *Majestic*, built in the 'nineties and considered obsolete when the war broke out, now lay upside down on the bottom of the Aegean. Obsolete maybe, but she served us well. We shall miss her protection. She was an inspiration to us all; how we cheered when her shells landed on Achi Baba. She had been our guardian. A quarter of an hour ago she was defiant and even now her keel had a look of defiance about it.

We now know why the warships and transports have gone.

A German submarine is lurking about – in a couple of days we have lost two battleships, HMS *Triumph* off Gaba Tepe and the *Majestic* off Cape Helles, thirteen miles to the south. A few days ago there were ships everywhere; now the *Majestic* has gone, we feel as though the Navy has deserted us.

Saturday, May 29th

We made an early morning start for the firing line, a long and tedious journey up the nullah, stopping and starting,, turning back and then forward again, tripping over wire, the incessant croaking of millions of frogs and the incredible accuracy of those well-concealed infernal snipers who score with every bullet.

It was a relief when we finally reached the firing line. It is not much of a trench but if you keep your head well down it affords reasonable cover. There are many gaps which are covered by the Turks. It is fatal to cross them, day or night.

We know this from experience. We at once set about closing these gaps by digging deeper but it was a painfully slow and dangerous task, especially in daylight.

CHAPTER SEVEN

JUNE

Tuesday, June 1st

We have bridged the gaps and made the trench in general much deeper. We can now move about much more easily and safely, which is just as well, as the Turks attacked but were beaten off. A few of them managed to penetrate our line but were easily dispatched. A feature of this attack was the accuracy of their shelling; time and again they scored direct hits. It was uncanny – they certainly had the range. More gaps meant more work and it took most of the rest of the day and night to repair the damage. The next day was quiet except for the shelling, which continued to be very accurate.

Thursday, June 3rd

We were relieved just before dawn. It was roughly about four o'clock when my crowd left the firing line. I was not sorry to leave as we had had a difficult spell. It was almost noon when we arrived back at our rest camp on the hill. Our remaining three battalions had landed during the nights of May 28th and 29th. They had received a more comfortable reception than we.

The Division was now complete in numbers of battalions and under our own General, Sir Archibald Paris. The newly arrived Hawke and Benbow Battalions joined Drake and Nelson to complete the First Naval Brigade and Collingwood, Hood, Howe and Anson Battalions made up the Second Naval Brigade. The Deal, Plymouth, Portsmouth and Chatham Battalions formed the Marine Brigade.

The arrival of these three fresh battalions will help to make up our losses but by no means cover them. We will still have less men than we had at the beginning of the campaign. Moreover, these men are wholly inexperienced. You cannot gain experience on the parade ground; in any case there are no parade grounds here. There is nothing here but flies, fighting and corpses. Every square yard is always under fire and, by the look of things, will remain so for some time to come. The Turks are firmly entrenched on the higher ground. We keep on nibbling at the cake – what else can we do but nibble, with the handful of men at our disposal? At least, now the Division will be operating under its own General in its own sector. Up to now we have been fighting on every sector of the front as loaned battalions. During the last month we have had as fighting companions Englishmen, Scots, Irish and Welsh of that wonderful 29th Division, Sikhs, Punjabis and Gurkhas in their light drill uniforms of Cox's Indian Brigade, Australians and New Zealanders, European French in their light blue, Senegalese in dark blue. Zouaves with their bright red trousers, Algerians, Goumiers and the heterogeneous elements that make up the Foreign Legion.

Join the Navy and see the World.' Join the Royal Naval Division and see the peoples of the World!

We talked of our experiences to the newcomers, – they were good listeners and were disappointed at having missed so much.

My goodness, they were anxious to get to the firing line. Poor fellows, they did not have to wait very long for at nine'o'clock in the evening we were on our way there, obviously for another attack. On we went, past the ruins of the old water towers which once carried a Roman aqueduct from the hills to Sedd-el-Bahr. We followed the watercourse past Skew Bridge and Backhouse Post and entered the communication trench just beyond the glade where many of our lads fell in the advance of May 6th. Colonel Quilter and Major Maxwell lie buried in this area. On still further we went past the white house and finally reached the firing line at two o'clock in the morning.

Friday, June 4th

Here we are back in the firing line, having left it only twenty-two hours previously. More than half the intervening time was spent in getting from and to the line. The line is very crowded — no hope for any rest – we simply – cannot move in any sector. Where everybody has come from, goodness only knows. There is not room to stand up in comfort, let alone sleep, and we could all do with some.

I was delighted when I and others were detailed to go back to Backhouse Post to bring up ammunition. We had completed one trip and with our second box of a thousand rounders were having a breather within a hundred yards or so of the firing line. The sun was terrifically hot and a thousand rounds of small arms ammunition is quite a heavy load. We were utterly exhausted and had only just sat down when a staff officer came along the trench and reminded us there was a war on. I know quite well. that the lower ranks must not speak to any officer unless the officer addresses him. I knew also that he was not speaking to me personally but, quite frankly, I didn't care. He was standing beside me so. I said that this was our second journey since six o'clock. 'Not bad, chaps, not bad at all Don't rest too long, will you?' and off he went on his way to the firing line with us at his heels. He soon outpaced us, though, as he was only carrying himself.

Arriving at the front line we reported to our company commander, Lieutenant-Commander Parsons.[1]

'Well done, men. We shall be all right now. If you wish you may stay in the trench with the garrison party when the advance begins at noon.'

I mentioned our meeting with the Staff Officer.

'Oh yes, that was Commodore Backhouse – charming fellow.'

The night, on the whole, had been quiet. At about eight to the morning our guns opened up and continued to bombard the Turkish trenches. At about eleven o'clock it seemed as though every gun on the Peninsula was firing – Turkish included. It was hell let loose. The sun shone pitilessly, the air was foul as the stench was by now sickening, and everywhere flies swarmed and maggots crawled – thousands of them from the dead bodies only inches below the soil. The scrub out in front was on fire and the smoke was choking us.

We still had another hour to wait before we advanced, It seemed years ago that the sun rose. Men were fast asleep on their feet and others were staring silently into the sides. The lad next to me checked his rifle and ammunition over and over again, still apparently not satisfied. Others just stood and waited, silent as the grave, maybe looking forward to it, who knows?

At eleven-thirty our guns ceased firing. Upon this half-hour's shelling depended the lives of many of us. Had this intensive bombardment

1 Lieutenant-Commander R. S. Parsons, RN. Killed Gallipoli June 4th, 1915.

disorganised the enemy trenches? Had it destroyed his machine-gun emplacements? Had the riflemen holding the trench been killed or driven to cover? At the moment we did not know. Everywhere was ghostly quiet except for the crackling of the burning scrub and grass. Even the Turks had ceased firing.

At a quarter-to-twelve we were ordered to show our bayonets above the parapet and to cheer loudly. A great and glorious cheer rang along the whole line as it to say: 'Look out, Johnnie. We are coming after you if there are any of you left' Or was it to tell them to hurry up and get those machine-guns in position? 'We will make an excellent target for you, and to make certain that you get the reception ready, we will not come for another fifteen minutes.'

We got our answer at once. The whole enemy line burst into rapid fire – machine-guns swept our parapet and their artillery blanketed our support trenches. They had not been destroyed, but were still there and quite ready for us.

The next fifteen minutes seemed like fifteen years. Our trench was about five feet deep. Commander Parsons was standing on one of the short ladders that were provided to enable us to get over the parapet, looking at his watch and then glancing at us beside him, with a comforting smile on his face.

'Five minutes to go, men.'

Then another glance at us – 'Four minutes... three minutes... two minutes... one minute, men. Are you all ready? Come on then, men, follow me.'

Over we went into the withering machine-gun fire. Poor old Lieutenant-Commander Parsons was killed in the first seconds and many fell back into the trench. The Turkish aim was perfect; Only a handful of us managed to cover the fifty yards to a stretch of dead ground immediately in front of us. We slowed down with the hope that we might be joined by others but there were none left to come.

With a mad rush we reached the Turkish front Line and jumped in. It must have been ten feet deep and was practically untouched. Where had all our shells gone? This was the first real Turkish trench I had seen and now I was in it I wanted to get out. I had to walk quite some distance before coming to a crater. At least one of those hundreds of shells had found its mark. I was thankful I was able, with others, to get out of this trap and to see several groups of our men advancing on the second trench which was clearly in sight. Soon we reached the parapet but we had no intention of diving into another trap. This was our objective and, having reached it, we set about filling it in so that we could see over the parados.

Whilst we remained outside we could see what the Turks were up to. At the moment they were taking pot-shots at us but. we had some protection from both the parapet and parados. Using our entrenching tools we tried to move the parapet into the trench but it appeared to be made mostly of dead bodies. We could not do much lying down but had to stand up; firing and digging alternatively like demons, trying to get some shelter from the bullets.

I suddenly felt as though someone had kicked me in the chest and can remember rolling over into the trench. I awoke later with a dreadful pain in the chest, a stiff face and able only to open one eye. I realised I was alone but, try as I might, I could not get to my feet.

'I must get out of here,' I kept telling myself. Seeing my rifle lying in the trench, just out of reach, I managed to crawl to it. Now I had hope and eventually got to my feet. Holding my rifle in front of me I walked slowly along the trench which, save for a few dead bodies, appeared to be empty, However, on rounding a traverse a bayonet thrust just caught my left wrist The formation of the trench and the fact that I had only one eye open had prevented me from seeing my attacker.

I waited a little and then moved forward again very cautiously until I was able to climb out of the trench. I saw in the distance my Platoon Commander, Sub-Lieutenant Cockey, and made my way towards him. He was alone, sitting on the parados, calmly sketching the Turkish trench system. I sat with him and, glancing back towards our own original line, was heartened by what I saw. There appeared to be three lines of men coming towards us.

They are the Collingwoods, sir.' I turned as I spoke, expecting confirmation from my officer, but he had gone. I looked in the trench for him but he had completely vanished. I remembered him saying something to me, but at the time I was having a shot at someone who was firing at me. He had drawn my notice to a particular clump of scrub and I was giving it my full attention as it was from that direction I was being fired on.

I felt very lonely but the Collingwoods were coming. They were going through us to capture the third trench. I remained outside and kept a good look-out and there were others doing the same – a group here and there and several solitary ones like me. I had fired several rounds and as I was not now being bothered I decided to refill my magazine. To my amazement I found that the whole of my ammunition was useless; my pouches were a mass of tangled cord and not a single round was undamaged. I extracted the bullet I had in the breech and examined my magazine – it was empty. I reloaded my only round. It then dawned on me what that kick in the chest had been and why I had come to be alone in the Turkish trench lying on top of a dead Turk. It was his blood, congealed by the sun, that had closed my eye.

Pouches are part of our equipment; a strap over each shoulder and fastened to the belt, holding ten pouches – five on either side – each holding three clips of five rounds. The pouches are held in position in front of the chest by the shoulder strap and belt. A hundred and fifty rounds of ammunition – very handy – and, in my case, very protective. It must have been a sweep of machine-gun fire that had caught me. Both groups of ammunition were shattered but what I didn't understand was how the gap of about six inches in between the two groups had been missed; also, why did none of the exploding cartridges penetrate my thick skin instead of making a fantastic criss-cross pattern of burnt lines across my chest and ribs. My tunic and shirt looked as though the moths had been at. them; they were much more 'holey' than I was up to that moment but this escape set me thinking.

One cannot dodge bullets, they somehow dodge you; but why? I think Lord Byron in his *Lines Addressed to a Young Lady* conveys exactly what I am trying to say:

> *Yes, in that nearly fatal hour*
> *The ball obey'd some hell-born guide;*
> *But Heaven, with interposing cower,*
> *In pity turned the death aside.*

I did not like the idea of fighting a battle single-handed with only one cartridge. There were plenty on the dead that were lying around. They had no further use for them. so I thought I would fill my pockets. With this object in view, I began to crawl towards the nearest body. In doing so I had to leave the shelter of the Turkish parapet.

The Collingwoods were still coming but there did not seem to be so many now – they were being mown down. I paused to think things out The firing was not coming from directly in front as I should be in the line of fire if it were. The bullets were coming from the direction of the Collingwoods. I crawled back to the trench for shelter and just short of the parapet tumbled into a small shell hole.

I could not counter-attack on my own with only a single cartridge. It seemed that if I stayed here my own crowd would get me. I could plainly see them firing, though not all at me.

Something had gone wrong, that was obvious. The Collingwoods, fresh from England, apparently thought there was no one between them and the Turks and, judging by the losses they were suffering, they had every right to think so.

For myself I was a bit fogged. I had advanced at noon with quite a crowd. Though not many reached the Turkish front line, there were quite a few of us who went forward and reached his second line. Others came up whilst we were there and then, after my pouches were exploded, I awoke to find myself alone. I then found and lost again Sub-Lieutenant Cockey. Where had everybody got to? There were only a handful of us scattered about here. We had reached our objective and had been ordered to stay here until the Collingwoods came up.

I had a perfect view from my shell hole but what I saw was distressing. Though the sun was scorching I felt cold and every bone in my body ached. I could see our lads falling and realised that very few of them would survive what must be a withering fire. But where was it coming from? Not a single man in my area, and my view was considerable, even reached the first Turkish line. If any had done so they must have crawled and I couldn't see them.

Poor old Collingwoods. Because they were fresh troops they got the blame in some quarters for the retirement This was most unfair. From what I saw, and swear by, the few that were left were still advancing when the extreme right fell back. It was the French that let us down; they caused the retirement, not the gallant Collingwoods. Our line was well ahead of the French before the advance began. They were supposed to advance fifteen minutes before us so that we would be in line but they never left their trenches with the result that we were subjected to enfilade fire from the Kereves Dere Ridge as soon as we moved forward. With our right flank in the air it was an impossible position. We should never have attempted to go forward until the French had come up into line. It was asking for trouble and we got it What a waste of human life, but this does not seem to be of any consequence.

The attack on the left of the Naval Division's sector carried out by the Howe Battalion was not very successful. Only a few of them succeeded in reaching the Turkish front line and the Turks were re-entering it.

With both flanks falling back, we in the centre went forward towards the enemy's third line but very few reached it. It was only a ditch. What a hopeless position we were in. The Turks were converging on the captured trenches from both flanks. I saw more Turks behind us than in front. There was no alternative but to fall back. We were being encircled and fired on from all directions. Those that were left of the Hood and Anson Battalions gave us the third trench. Upon reaching the second trench, isolated groups spread themselves out and prepared to make a stand on this line but the trench was much too deep to be of any use to us. The right flank continued to fall back and we had to give up more of our hard-won ground.

The tragedy of it all was that we also had to give up our dead and dying. It is heart-rending to leave a man to die of his wounds in 'No man's land' under the scorching sun, but there is absolutely nothing anyone can do except give the hurried advice: 'Come on, lad, we are retiring' – knowing full well he cannot heed you. You pick your way over the dead as if you were crossing a stream by way of stepping stones. A few yards run, then you lie down with the dead, using their bodies for shelter. Another short run and you again bury your head like an ostrich. A single blade of grass is shelter to a fugitive from death.

The original Turkish front line was only about twenty yards away. I decided to crawl the rest of the way. I could rest a while when I reached it. Maybe some of our men were there and intended to hold on to it I felt very sorry we had had to give up so much ground. The Turks did not appear to be pressing their counter-attack in the centre; all the firing was coming from the flank. If there were enough of us we could hold on.

I continued my crawl to within a couple of yards and, rising with the intention of jumping into the trench, I was thunder-struck to find it full of Turks. I made a flying leap over the top, helped by a Turkish bayonet which jabbed me in the base of my spine and sent me sprawling headlong into a shell-hole in front of the parapet I was afraid to move as I was less than six feet in front of a trench full of Turks.

Waiting for the end, I said my prayers hurriedly. I asked God for protection and thought of the effect my demise would have on Mother. I knew poor Tom's[1] death had almost killed her.

Now it was me – any second now. I asked God to save me for her sake; I asked this not only once but as often and quickly as I could. I asked whether I should stand up and fight for my life or whether I should crawl away or remain where I was. I had to know quickly. I pleaded not to be allowed to be taken prisoner; that would be a living death.

I was lying on my rifle and moved my hand slowly along the barrel until

1 Thomas Murray. Lost HMS *Good Hope* November 1st, 1914.

I was able to grip the trigger. I had only one round and had to be sure of making full use of it if the occasion arose. I was more settled now. I had been there for at least a minute and was still alive. I could see the flashes from the Turkish rifles as they fired and smell the cordite or whatever powder they used. Every bone in my body ached but I dared not move. Just above my head a Turkish rifle was continually being fired through a loophole in the parapet; the resulting fumes nauseated me but I was afraid to be sick. I anxiously watched it being sighted, then heard the crack, and so it went on everlastingly. The marksman could not see me and I could easily have grabbed the barrel but that would have been fatal.

I had asked God for protection. I realised now that my prayers were being answered and I was comforted. But I must help myself by remaining motionless. I was being baked by the sun; my drinking water had long since gone, but for this I was thankful as, with such a thirst, I doubt it I could have resisted trying to reach it. Watching the rifle barrel carefully and judging its movements, I managed, by pressing my face into the loose, sandy soil, to get a stone into my mouth. Unfortunately some sand got into my nose and this was most irritating. The stone eased my thirst but my nose drove me crazy – and that rifle-crack, crack, crack-would it ever stop?

My only hope of escape was in the coming darkness; even my borrowed time seemed long. I felt as it I had spent a lifetime there, yet it was still very bright and tremendously hot. The sun was slowly going down, however, and I had the consolation that it gets dark in a hurry out here, there being very little dusk. I felt that it must get dark soon.

I moved my legs a little. I was awfully cramped but I must be able to move when the time came. I was sure it was getting dark now but I must still wait. The thought of the coming darkness filled me with hope. I would cheat them after all.

As the firing had eased considerably, I got a little more venturesome. My pet rifle had not fired for some time. I watched it being drawn in out of sight and believed in my crazy mind that the owner was being relieved. Would his relief look over the top of the parapet instead of using the loophole? If he did, all would be up with me.

The sweat was pouring from me but I realised that I must not panic. I told myself he could not look over the parapet as the trench was much too deep to allow it. Hours ago I had traversed quite a lot of this trench and even when I had stood on the fire-step, I could not see over the top. Perhaps he was taller than I? But why should he look over the top when he had a safe loophole to use. They were much safer than ours as they do not face the immediate front but arc slantwise. A clever method of construction as a frontal shot at them would do no damage at all, whereas with ours the enemy can observe the flash and score a deadly shot through them. I have seen it happen many times. The Turkish marksmanship is incredible. We only use our loopholes in daylight and look over the top when it is dark.

My excursion into the Turk's trench has left me wondering how be manages in the dark. He must use the loopholes all the time. Maybe he has some special look-out posts, but though I have traversed well over a hundred yards of his trench, I have not noticed any.

I did notice, though, that it was getting dusk and that my pet rifle had not fired for quite some time. It was very quiet and strange – it was uncanny and I was disturbed. I began to wonder if the constant cracking of that menacing rifle had made me deaf.

The silence was broken by a strange chanting in the trench. Was I really hearing this chanting or was I going crazy? I could not believe my ears and closed my eyes to help me to concentrate. I could recognise the intonation; was it an exhortation to attack? I clutched my rifle firmly; I was really scared and in a semi-panic. I knew I had moved a little – the first real movement for hours. Had I been indiscreet? I was still alive but fancied I was being watched. Any more movement would be fatal.

I again asked for God's protection; simultaneously I heard the Turks asking Allah. They too were praying – it must be sunset. For a moment I did not know what to do. 'Allah, Allah' was ringing in. my ears. I hoped their Keblah was in the opposite direction to me. As they turn. their faces to Mecca during prayer, this was my one and only chance to crawl away. I hoped. My belief that they are very devout in their prayers was correct.

I glanced to see if that rifle was there – it was not. Slowly I eased myself away and paused for a second to wonder if I should wait until it was really dark. Darkness was not many minutes away but if the Turks' prayers were over they would hear my movements. I must go now or never.

I crawled out of my shell-hole at a snail's pace; I was too numb to do otherwise even if I wanted to. I could still hear the chanting and thanked God for it. I quickened my pace and the chanting topped – so did I. I felt I should have made more of my chance and was angry with myself. I should now have to wait for the darkness and had not the shelter of the shell-hole but at least I was away from the Turks' parapet. There were yards instead of feet between us.

Now that glorious chanting – even louder than ever – was again ringing in my ears, or was it my fancy? I knew I was not clear in my head as I could not focus things correctly. I heard things that I knew were not real and saw people that were not there – they could not be as some of them were dead. My mother was three thousand miles away, yet she was there with me most of the time. When she left I was very lonely, feeling I had said or thought something to displease her – I didn't mean to.

Louder and louder the chanting went on and quicker and quicker I crawled away from it. I could feel blood on my knees and on my hands but I had to continue. I felt that if I could manage another twenty yards I would have a reasonable chance at living. I struggled on but was so tired. I wanted to sleep. I thought I was now about midway between the two trenches and decided to wait until it was really dark. I think I must have slept a little then as, when I awoke, it was very dark. I began my crawl; it would have been quicker to run and much less painful but I doubted if I could walk, let alone run.

I was now much more afraid of my own men than of the Turks. Nearing our own line I called out – not too loudly – but got no response. I called again, with the same negative result so I crawled on but a bullet struck the sand quite close to me. I called again and another bullet struck the sand. Frantically I got to my feet and attempted to run, but crashed among the scrub. I called out my name and battalion again and again, and after what seemed ages, I was answered. I was instructed to wait.

'What the hell for; I've been waiting all day.'

'You wait until I tell you to come in,' was the reply.

I had a real chance of living now, I thought, but Johnnie Turk had something to say about that. He opened up rapid fire and I had to wait until he had satisfied himself that he had beaten off yet another attack. Fortunately the firing did not last long and when it died down I was called from the trench to make a dash for it and bear a little to the right. I did this and one short dash was enough to bring me back to the trench I had left, full of hope, at twelve noon. Holding this bay were only four unwounded men – the rest were either dead or dying, killed as they were leaving at noon to attack or, having survived the machine-gun fire for a second, had crawled back to the trench to die. The floor of the trench was three or four deep with bodies. They were slumped on the fire step and hanging over the parapet, some head-first as they had died of their wounds or had been riddled with bullets as they were trying to make their escape. Of others, only their legs could be seen, their bodies lying over the parapet. They were just beginning and ending what historians in years to come and war correspondents on the spot (which means to a warship a couple of miles off-shore) will refer to as the glorious charge of the illustrious Royal Naval Division on the fourth of June.

We could have pulled the bodies to but there just wasn't room for them. We were standing now on our dead comrades; left where they were, they served the requirements of the living; they were providing us with that little extra cover and compensating a little for the loss occasioned by their deaths.

Our trench, once cut through the soil, was now a narrow passage through human flesh, bones and blood. The communication trench was so full of bodies that it could not be used to get the wounded out. They had been patched up with all the available dressings, but a couple of bandages is not much use when an arm or a leg has been shattered and many would bleed to death.

Had the Turks known our sorry plight, we would have been at their mercy. If they had only known, they could have overrun our sector and broken the line. The actual battle had lasted for forty-five minutes. The Second Naval Brigade advanced on a front of less than a thousand yards with roughly two thousand men and seventy officers. Only nine hundred and fifty men and five officers returned. More than half of us had been killed and we had not gained one inch of ground.

Now that I was back to the trench I exchanged my tunic with a chap who had finished with his. I also helped myself to his equipment. He had not fired a single round but had drunk quite a lot of water. I filled my mouth with some that was left and held it there as my throat was so dry that I was unable to swallow. After a few moments I spat most of it out on to a piece of khaki rag and bathed my eye open. It was a great relief to be able to see again. I was now quite refreshed and felt a new man.

We could not tidy the trench as we had to keep on the fire-step. There was considerable firing going on away over to our left but we were not unduly bothered, which was all the more reason why we must keep our eyes open. I had crawled through the scrub for three or four hundred yards so the Turks could do the same. We must be forever watchful.

I found it most difficult to keep awake. Staring into the darkness hour after hour, the whole scene appeared to be alive. The stones have eyes and stare back at you and the dead change places with each other. I could plainly see two bodies where for hours I had seen only one.

My eyelids closed – I could not resist their falling – my eyes were asleep but my mind was fully awake, not so much to the present moment but to the hours that had passed, and to my brief cogitation I wondered how my pals had fared. The battle speech from *Henry V* came to my mind:

> *He that outlives this day and comes safe home*
> *Will stand a tip-toe when this day is named.*

How many will be in the muster; how many of us will come safely home? 'One crowded hour of glorious life is worth an age without a name,' says Sir Walter Scott in *Marmion*. Maybe in a history book that is so but, after the war is over, what will be its worth to a man who is disabled for life and has to compete with his more fortunate brothers who stayed at home to wave the flags?

Saturday, June 5th

It was almost daybreak before we were relieved by the Hawke Battalion of the First Naval Brigade and we came back to support. Actually we were in the second line, about fifty yards nearer the beach, and this eased the strain. There was none of that constant look-out, but one was always at the-ready. Still, there was time to munch a biscuit in comparative comfort and to dig a small hole with the hope that a little water might trickle in during our stay. One never knew when we would be able to get the next bottle of water. Nothing is certain here, least of all life, but we live to hope and prepare for the coming hours and what they might bring.

I was a bit lonely now as most of my pals were gone. Out of my section of twelve men, one petty officer and a leading seaman, I knew that eight were dead; Petty Officer Warren, Able Seamen Yates, Horton, Packwood, Aston, Kelly, Mutch and Buckley. My pal Tubby, had also left me, having gone back to the rear without a thumb. I had watched him put it over the muzzle of his own rifle and pull the trigger in sheer panic. Poor chap, he was prancing about like a cat on hot bricks. I caught hold of him with much difficulty and began to bandage him up. The blood was squirting out like a fountain. As soon as I had bandaged what was left of his thumb, the whole lot collapsed, we decided it would be better to cut off altogether what was left The bone and the major part of the flesh had already gone. What remained would be of no earthly use and if we didn't stop the bleeding quickly, it wouldn't be necessary to do so. I have a jack-knife as sharp as any Service-issue razor. I'm very proud of my knife. Service-issue knives, as a rule, are all right for opening jam tins, but won't cut butter; they don't get the chance to out here, but that is by the way. My knife is different to this. It has a very large blade and a marlin spike so, with Tubby's approval, I began the operation in cold blood, like a butcher cutting up the Sunday joint. Tubby howled like the devil – he is only a youngster, not yet nineteen. Come to think of it, he is older than me! Well, I pushed and sawed for all I was worth but, try as I might, could not sever the offending flesh. By now Tubby had lost a lot of blood. Something had to be done quickly and the alternative was to try chopping it off. I placed the thumb on the butt of his rifle, inserted the blade and, with a sharp tap with my fist, the operation was complete. Bandaging was now a simple matter; the flies were the only trouble as they would not go away and had to be included in the dressing.

With this bloody business over, we both sat down. Tubby thanked me a thousand times. He said he just could not stand any more. He was afraid we would have to attack those trenches again and he had the wind up. With tears streaming down his grimy cheeks he pleaded with me not to split on him.

A short while ago I could have slit his throat much more easily than I had his thumb and with considerably less effort but now, somehow, I had a different focus. I was angry – very angry indeed. We had been together all the way through and now we must part through his own efforts. We considered how to explain the powder marks on the remains of his thumb and agreed to say that just before the attack, to the excitement someone fired a rifle as Tubby was climbing out of the trench. This would be his account of what happened. I made a similar statement later on, when asked.

That was the last I saw of Tubby; he never bothered to write to me. I know he got to England and was discharged. His brother was in my company and we often met. I told him it was an accident, but I know he did not believe me. He was a good soldier and I wouldn't have hurt him for the world.

Sunday, June 6th

We were back once more to our rest camp, beat to the world, We actually rested until late afternoon when we assembled for a working party. Hardly enough to form a football team, the feeble veterans of a former throng moved off towards the beach, helped on our way by a few shrapnel bursts overhead. Asiatic Annie was shelling 'W' Beach and it was in that direction we were heading.

I cannot understand why our rations are so meagre. One would have thought that as our numbers are reduced to less than half each time we leave the firing line there would be additional rations, at least for a day or two, but they seem to get less. Surely they don't cut the ration requirements on the assumption that we shall need only half the previous amount as only half will return each time? I did not think it was possible for man to exist, let alone live, on such meagre portions of fly-infested oily cheese, a few hard biscuits and a daily billy-can of bully beef stew flavoured with millions of blue-black flies. I don't know what the other troops get but this is all we have, My stomach aches for food and aches even more after I have eaten the food that is given me.

We ambled on and finally reached 'W' Beach, the place where the sea ends and the land begins. Once there was a little sand; now it is a scrap-iron dump to the middle of a horse and mule fair. Each animal has a host of attendants, or so it would seem from the number of nicely-bronzed chaps that are here-abouts; we could do with a few of them a couple of miles inland. I know they don't know where the firing line is, but we know it well – too well in fact We would be pleased in act as expert guides.

At the foot of the cliff there was a queue of about a hundred waiting for a swarthy Greek to open up his canteen. We were hanging around waiting to be told what to do. It seems that these beach-wallahs order as many working parties, as they can get. They have to justify their jobs I suppose, and the more men they have the greater importance is attached to their tasks. They strut about with an air of absolute to dispensability whilst we wait – half asleep – for orders.

I decided that I could wait in the queue quite as easily as here so, choosing the right moment to slide off, I joined it Had I asked for permission it would certainly not have been given; no one ever has the authority to do anything sensible. So I just faded away; everyone knew, of course, but no one worried. The only point at issue was that no one actually gave me permission.

Only Asiatic Annie made any protest. She does not like a half-starved, half-baked ghost trying to get something extra to eat. The 'waiting for work' party and the queue scattered, so did the bones of former young men that fell to the pride of their youth and were buried where they fell. There was only an occasional shell but each one stirred up the past. As the smoke cleared and the queue reformed, the next shell made a direct hit on the pier. This amused us as men had been carrying rocks to it all afternoon to repair previous damage.' Now they would have to start repairing this latest damage – and so the war goes on.

The canteen queue formed again and I was much nearer to the still unopened door, but my advanced position to the line in no way worried me. Being in front of a queue is much healthier than being in front of a firing squad, as I have been of late.

With apologies to the nursery rhyme – 'When the door was opened, the flies began to hum'. The dainty dish set before the king was a dozen or so figs on a string. I asked for a tin of condensed milk. The Greek made his face even uglier than it normally was and, with a characteristic shrug of his shoulders, offered me a string of figs. It was Hobson's choice, figs or nothing. Lovely juicy chunks of dysentery, covered with the usual layers of flies. I came away delighted; however bad they were they would certainly be easier on the teeth than the biscuit diet.

My crowd had not done much work; what had been done the shell had undone in much less time and with less effort. Our job was to unload lighters and one had now arrived alongside the pier. The same old stunt was used – carry a box from the lighter and return with a lump of rock to drop in the sea and forget you ever saw it. Mind you, a box often gets broken in transit. A nicely broken box of condensed milk can and does fall into the sea. A good wash is good for the soul at times. In about ten feet of water the pearl divers of the Far East have nothing on as. We can locate a box of milk with unfailing ease, pick out a single tin, jab two holes in the top with our marlinspikes – and suck a mixture of milk and salt water, enjoying every drop.

It was an unwritten law that whoever had the broken box must fall in the sea. He was lucky as he knew of its whereabouts and had first go. The others had to search for the box but as a rule we were all satisfied with our day at the seaside, The occasional stolen feed might have to last us a week or even longer.

I must make it plain to my reader that this business only operated between the lighters and the beach. Rations carried from the Quartermaster's Store to the front line always got there intact. It is true that biscuits were in sealed tins but cheese, bacon, tea, sugar and the inevitable apricot jam could become 'lost' but never were. That would be sacrilege. We would trudge through what seemed to be miles of trenches to deliver the rations to the lads in the line. They did the same for us but, even so, it seemed to be a wasted effort to carry tea and sugar, mixed in a sandbag, to the firing line. You have to have water to make tea and the lads had precious little. Then again, hot water is needed. I have often stolen over between the trenches near the firing line, cutting myself to shreds to collect stinking prickly scrub for a fire and then spent hours blowing and blowing at the smouldering embers until I could see nor blow no longer, and never once managed to boil a milk tin of water. In the rest camp I could manage it, but there was always a shout of 'Stop making that smoke!' At night it was: 'Turn out that light!' Of course, all this is understandable as we were always in full view of the Turks. The only things they could not see were the empty milktins to the sea near the pier though they disturbed them on many occasions.

On the whole, the working parties were not too bad. They more or less alternated between the beach and the front line or the support line with trench-digging during me hours of darkness. Each day someone was either killed or wounded. Sometimes we would have a bad spell – a machine-gun burst or a shell would land among us and we would lose a dozen or so – but these incidents had no fixed pattern. We would be out to the open all night digging a communication trench under the Turk's very nose and not suffer a single casualty, yet on the way back, maybe a mile to the rear, a shrapnel shell would burst overhead and wipe out a whole group. Such are the fortunes of war.

Saturday, June 19th

All day yesterday we were busy preparing to leave camp. We have made several trips to 'V' Beach and rumour has it that we are going to be relieved – these trips to 'V' Beach augur well During the evening parties from Hood, Howe and Anson Battalions left for Imbros, an island lying a little off the west coast – about a two-hour run. They took with them all they had in the world. I and five men from Benbow Battalion have been looking after the stores. We would follow later – at least, that's what we thought I was not perturbed but fancy leaving me to look after stores.

I was the odd man out and apparently nobody's child. I was the only one left of the 1st Section, 9th Platoon, 'C' Company. and seemed to get the odd jobs but I didn't mind this one. As I am the old soldier of the party, the Benbow chaps not having landed until the end of May, I was recognised as being in charge.

What was left of the battalion had gone for a rest so why shouldn't we have a rest? We arranged for a sentry during the day and a two-man patrol at night One would imagine it was the Bank of England we were guarding instead of heaps of picks and shovels and a grimy field kitchen. Still we were on guard duty and everything had to be done according to the book of regulations. We arranged some of the boxes to form our guard room and, having detailed the night patrols, settled down for the night

Monday, June 21st

We had breakfast very early and three men then volunteered to look after the picks and shovels whilst the others decided on a bit of scrounging for something extra to eat. The French seem always to have plenty to eat so we made our way to their lines. We had had such a tuck-in for breakfast that we had to get something somewhere.

Without much effort we were soon amongst the French on the extreme right and our luck was in. We collected almost a sackful of nearly black bread; it was very hard but was the first bread I had seen since leaving the ship. We drank more red wine than we should have done – the Senegalese fellows really made a fuss of us.

During our visit they decided to attack the Haricot Redoubt and I believe they met with considerable success. They had to leave us hurriedly and, by the number of wounded coming back, they were evidently hard-pressed. They held on to their gains whilst we had the support trench to ourselves. We didn't want it, but there was so much old iron flying about that we had no alternative but to wait for a while. In fact, we were forced to look for better cover and, in doing so, found several more pieces of stale bread. It would have been wicked to leave them to waste; we could soak them and, mixed with a dollop of apricot jam, raw roly-poly pudding would be on the menu. I would have thanked the French quarter-master before we left but, as there was fighting going on, we could not find him.

It was very late when we reached our precious shovels. The sentry on duty reported 'All picks and shovels correct, sir'. The bread was placed to an empty box and I, as unpaid officer-in-charge, gave instructions to the night patrol that it must be guarded with their lives. They must not on any account leave it unattended. If the box was missing to the morning I, personally, would shoot them both at sunrise. Fearing death to the morning, the patrol made sure of living by sleeping on the box. We all slept well and, incidentally, had a jolly good breakfast

Sunday, June 27th

The battalion re-landed on the Peninsula from Imbros, fully reorganised, whatever that signified. They looked better for their rest and not so ghostly. They all agreed that they felt better. Apparently 'Reveille' had been at 5 am, parade at 6 and work until 8.20; breakfast 8.30 to 9.30 and parade again at 9.30 to 10.30. The rest of the day was free until 5 pm, when there was an hour's work until 6 – except on Friday, 25th,' when they were inspected by Sir Ian' Hamilton who had a few kind words for them. It was the usual 'Fine body of men!..,' etc.

Monday, June 28th

We have resumed our general working parties, sometimes on the beaches and at other times digging in the forward positions. There is an attack going on and the left centre, the 29th and 52nd Divisions, have moved forward. We are not involved, though we have had to take shelter from the shrapnel and bullets overshooting their marks.

Tuesday, June 29th

Another attack was made today but this time it was the French who were attacking on the extreme right.

CHAPTER EIGHT

JULY

Saturday, July 3rd

We have been out in the open tonight, trying to dig a trench across a gap. It is almost solid rock. We made an awful lot of noise and repeatedly had to lie down as the Turks, hearing the noise, swept the entire front with rifle and machine-gun fire. Most of it was high overhead but, even so, our little group lost two dead and two wounded.

Sunday, July 4th

A day at the seaside for a change. We have been cutting steps to the cliffs between 'W' and 'X' Beaches to be used for storing shells. Some French Colonials were being landed by motor boats from a large transport lying quite a distance offshore. We were admiring the fine ship and inwardly wishing we were on board, but changed our minds when she began to sink stem first. In less than three minutes she was perpendicular, with her bows high in the air. She seemed to remain in that position for quite a while before she plunged out of sight beneath the calm surface of the sea. I did not hear any explosion. Only two or three boat-loads from her have landed, unless there have been others which I haven't seen, but I doubt it I fear many men must have been lost as there would not have been time to

Imperial Forces advancing through the thick bush of German East Africa

Horses and equipment being unloaded at 'V' beach

The climb from the beaches on the Gallipoli Peninsula

Soldiers swimming south of the 'X' beach

Barges & Tow, ANZAC 1915

British soldiers firing a Howitzer from positions a Helles

The landing at Suvla Bay, August 1915

The beached River Clyde

Advance across No-Man's-Land

No. 4 Gun, 9th Battery, McClay's Ridge, Gallipoli

Moving of supplies in autumn 1915

Australian stationary hospital at North Beach, Anzac Cove

Men from the Royal Naval Division and the Australian Citizen Army operating a periscope rifle at Anzac

Guns and soldiers being evacuated from Suvla by raft, December 19th, 1915

Turkish bodies on No Man's land in front of the Anzac positions

launch many boats. It was all over in a matter of minutes.

I later heard that the ship was the *Carthage*. Rather an appropriate name, I think.

Monday, July 5th

Today will always be remembered by the lads of the Royal Naval Division as the day the Turks pinched the Ansons' breakfast. The Turks attacked at the junction of the Anson line with that of the French and about fifty of them managed to get into the Anson firing line but an immediate counter attack easily drove them out.

It all happened so quickly that the officer in charge of that particular sector; on coming out of his dugout after finishing his breakfast, had to be told that the Turks had paid him a visit whilst he had been enjoying his meal.

Of course, after this episode, if we met any of the Anson lads we always enquired if they had had any breakfast.

It has been a sorry day for the Turks. According to the Anson chaps, they were being urged forward by a couple of German officers. It is fatal to hesitate between the lines. There was no hesitation on the part of the machine-gunners of Drake and Hawke Battalions.

Tuesday, July 6th

A change is as good as a rest and today I have had a change. I was included in a party of twenty-four from the Hood Battalion loaned to the Divisional Engineers. A few days ago men with any knowledge of mining had been asked for and I put my name down.

It was early evening when we reached the Engineers' dump to a small gully. They were having a concert when we arrived. What a change, A good laugh and a cup of cocoa – the first since leaving the *Grantully Castle*. It was a treat. The evening was as cool and refreshing as the cocoa but I wonder what happened to the cocoa for our mob. If the Engineers could get cocoa, why could not the fighting men?

We were awakened at 5 am, and after a breakfast consisting of tea, a slice of fried bacon and a couple of three-inch-square biscuits, we set off for the support lines at 6 am, armed with picks and shovels.

The Engineer chap led six of us out into the open ground between the forward and support trenches. It was dead ground and we walked about unseen. With the exception of a few stray bullets which appeared to be high over our heads, we were left unmolested.

The Engineer marked out a square which he said was to be a gun pit and detailed four men for the job. A man called Jones and I and the Engineer moved back about thirty yards or so where we began sinking a well. I was put in charge of both the gun pit and the well. It was a soft job, we thought, and our' well began to take shape. The soil was easily dug for tile first few or five feet and we had room to get rid of it away from the top.

Everything went like a song until eight o'clock when a burst of shrapnel killed two and seriously wounded the other two on the gun pit site. Jones and I went over to investigate the damage. We carried the wounded to a nearby trench and then went back for the other two. We were determined that they should be buried as there were so many that had already fallen in the open and remained unburied. Now we are committed to trench warfare, they could lie there for months. We dragged their bodies back to the trench only to find that both the wounded had died.

The Engineer chap came to see how we were getting on. He was obviously distressed and said he would arrange for the burial. With this assurance we continued with the well. So much for our soft job! Within two hours, four out of the six of us were dead. It was the only shell that fell anywhere near us the whole day. The gun site was not visible. It was just one of those things we cannot grasp.

Saturday, July 10th

After four days' work on the well and not finding a single drop of water even at fifteen feet, we were given a new job. This was to dig a short trench to be used as a bombing sap from the firing line towards that of the Turk. We had plenty of help from the lads in the line and they soon got rid of the soil we dug. We went forward as an open trench for about ten yards and. then began to tunnel underneath, leaving roughly eighteen inches of soil as roof cover. The idea was that during the night this roof could be broken down and we would be that much nearer to the Turkish line, thus enabling us to sling our jam-tin bombs into his line with much less effort. Of course he would be in exactly the same position as regards to us.

I was quite pleased that we were going underneath as we would have shelter. Our reliefs would arrive in about an hour, anyway. The infantrymen who followed us made the trench quite deep. They took advantage of the cover we had given them and about a dozen, working in pairs, soon had a very good bombing sap. For some reason our artillery opened up and, of course, the Turks followed suit. It had been quite peaceful all day but within a matter of minutes the Turks scored several direct hits on our front line including our new trench at a point behind where we were digging. We were quite safe in our advanced cubby-hole but could not get back to the firing line.

The shelling ceased after about half an hour. We could hear the men digging beyond the blockage and had no cause to cease our own efforts underneath as the more we dug, the more cover we had.

Our reliefs should have arrived by now but the shelling had obviously delayed them. Maybe it was them that we could hear digging on the other side but the shelling had ceased over an hour ago and the digging was not getting any nearer. We decided to start clearing the trench from our side. Whilst we had plenty of room to move about we were very exposed when clearing the debris. We therefore had to keep very low and the risk did not seem worthwhile but we felt we must do something. As it turned out, it was a good job we did continue for after a while I heard someone calling and, by the tone of his voice, the caller did not expect an answer. I called back at once and his next call was to a much more hopeful tone.

'How many of you are there?'

'Two second-hand engineers,' I replied.

'Good. Look out, I'm coming over,' and sure enough the engineer fellow crawled over the debris, like a snake, to broad daylight.

It was a most welcome visit and we felt that we were back to circulation. We thanked him for risking his skin in order to join us; His face beamed with delight. He said he had been told we had been buried with the rest of them. This was news to us; It appeared that several men had been buried in the trench and the men in the firing line had erected a barricade in the damaged part of our bombing sap, believing the rest to be destroyed. All the time we had thought they were trying to free us, they were building another obstacle for us to climb.

With our visitor the time seemed to pass quickly. We seem to get into a mess during the daylight and then have to wait for nightfall to extricate ourselves. It was almost dark when the Infantrymen came over to occupy our end of the sap and others had almost cleared the rest of it.

Back at base, the lads had made tea and shared what was left with us. We felt that almost a whole day had been wasted but we would make up for the loss tomorrow, that is, if the Turks allowed.

Sunday, July 11th

We were back in the bombing sap at 8.30 a.m. and noticed that the men had made a good job of clearing away the debris. We had only just begun from where we had left off yesterday when we were recalled to the firing line to begin another sap of a different type. We had to cut it step fashion as soon as we got under the parapet I have never seen any of this type before but it was quite obvious that they were to assist the troops in getting out of the trench quickly. On June 4th we had to use short ladders but these step ramps would enable the men to rush out.

We thought that an attack must be imminent as these openings were a potential danger to the men occupying the line. All the sappers were engaged on these saps. The line was occupied by the 52nd Division. We were told that the object of the impending attack would be the same as on June 4th but with greater hope of success because those Turkish positions on Kerevcs Dere Ridge that were responsible for the enfilade fire which had almost wiped out the Second Naval Brigade had been captured by the French on June 21st.

Our artillery has been sending hundreds of shells these last two days. Even while we were digging, two warships were bombarding the Turkish positions.

We left the line at dusk and made our way back to our base in the gully. During the meal we were warned to be back in the Line early on the morrow, so we slept.

Monday, July 12th

Back to the firing line, today we are on the right of the 52nd Division and hear the French. I somehow seem to be attracted to them.

Shortly after 6 am the artillery increased its tempo. To me, this was by far the heaviest bombardment I had heard on the Peninsula. I was very pleased indeed as when I last went over the top out of this same trench we had only a desultory bombardment all morning, with a quarter of an hour's break and then a final quarter of an hour of heavy shelling. This morning's bombardment was much more intense.

We had lots of tidying up to do which kept us busy until the troops were assembled and waiting for the signal to attack. At 7.30 am. the French and the right of the 52nd Division went forward. This should have been the order of things on June 4th, but then the French did not move. Later on this morning, the centre and the left also moved forward. The fresh 52nd Division recaptured those trenches we had captured but lost again on June 4th. I hoped that they could hold on to them, and that as the French had gone forward with them this time, there should not be that deadly enfilade fire. The Turks would not be able to get behind the advanced troops as they had with us.

Things appeared to be going well. Many wounded returned to the firing line and we assisted them into the trench, giving first-aid by bandaging them up as best we knew how and showing them the way to the communication trench.

It is a strange feeling to be left in the trench when an attack is to progress. It was unusual for me to be left behind and, quite frankly, I didn't like it a bit. Bullets were flying overhead and 'there was a lot of shrapnel. In a deep trench like this you feel out of touch with what is going on; you wonder if the attack is succeeding or if the lads are being held up. The returning wounded can only tell you what was happening to their little area up to the time they left. More and more troops were going forward which was a hopeful sign. Even so, this could mean anything. On June 4th we in the centre were going forward at the same time as the right flank – only three hundred yards away – were retiring. Today it appeared that the lads had captured those three trenches.

The firing has died down quite a lot There was an urgent call for ammunition from the captured trenches. Everyone available had to take it forward and this included me. What a rotten job – a thousand times worse than going forward to the initial attack. We struggled forward for what seemed hours before we reached the second captured trench. This was the limit of the advance at this spot though there were many of our men out in front. There was confusion everywhere and no one knew anything. There did not appear to be any more trenches; if there were, I could not see them.

This was not my fight but it seemed safer to stay in the new firing line than to risk going back, so there I stayed. I was in good company – mostly men of the King's Own Scottish Borderers with a few of the Highland Light Infantry to help them out. I should have been a mile to the rear but, judging by the shells that were going over that way, I was much better off staying put – at least for the time being.

Still more men joined us. The trench here is fairly deep. It was knocked about in places but we made a fire-step and settled down quite comfortably. I took my turn at look-out and managed a little rest as darkness fell, firing broke out again on our left – the centre of the divisional front. Things did not appear to be quite right there, but after a while it became quiet again and we got on with the job of consolidating our position.

Tuesday, July 13th

During the night we had made our trench very respectable but in the morning we were extremely amazed to see some of the HLI men retiring on our left. There was a lot of rifle fire but the Turks were not attacking. Were we, as on June 4th, going to lose all we had gained? It was that deadly enfilade fire that had caused the retirement then, but not today. The French were in line with us, so why this retirement?

This Achi Baba Nullah must be haunted; throughout the day we held on knowing that all was not well on our immediate left. There appeared to be a gap to the centre; the extreme left was well advanced and we on the right appeared to be ahead of the centre. Tormented by the sun and flies, with the stench making us sick, there was nothing we could do but wait.

Late in the afternoon firing broke out again in the centre. The Portsmouth Marines came up in fine style and when they were level with us we went forward with them to search of that mysterious third trench but although we covered some considerable distance, we failed to find it. We were much too far ahead and were ordered to retire to a more suitable position in front of a shallow ditch, which could have been mistaken for the third trench. On our way back we saw the bodies of many King's Own Scottish Borderers lying about where they had fallen yesterday. The firing was now as intense as ever and there were dead and dying everywhere. This miserable piece of scrubland has been paid for over and over again: this continual nibbling is getting us absolutely nowhere and is costing us the youth of Britain. We have beaten the Turk to his knees time and time again but never have enough men left to follow up our success. We have to wait until a few are available but if we could only have a couple of fresh divisions we could overrun that mocking bill to a single day. The divisions that have arrived do not make up for the losses sustained to the battle that always precedes their arrival The 42nd were available after the battle of May 6th, the 52nd after the battle of June 4th, and now mat they have suffered very heavy losses, any new division will again only partly make them up. And so, with a handful of half-starved, sick and battle-weary men whose courage alone enables them to walk to and from the firing Line, we go on trying to defeat an army deeply entrenched in a natural fortress. It is pitiful to see men, not long ago strong and healthy, now with drawn faces and staring eyes, struggling towards the firing line. Most of them should be in hospital. They are cheating death but only just. They are walking corpses – the ghosts of Gallipoli.

Wednesday, July 14th

During the night the Drake Battalion came and filled the gap to the centre. We now have a continuous line, so they say. The firing has more or less ceased and we are ready for a counter-attack should one develop.

Just before dawn I left the line and made my way back to my own unit further down the Nullah. It was well into the afternoon when I arrived at the dump to learn that most of the sappers had, in some form or another, been involved in the attack. Most had been able to return during the night of the 12th but there were still four to come.

I was ravenously hungry and very tired. I was excused duty for the rest of the day and allowed to sleep until breakfast the next day, when I was included to the party that was to sink wells. Just the job for me – fit as a fiddle after the best sleep I had had since landing.

We set off towards the beach to a spot in the low-lying ground about a mile inland from 'W' Beach but less than a quarter of a mile from 'X' Beach. The Engineer marked out where the well was to be and left us to get on with the job.

Friday, July 16th

On our way across this huge graveyard we came upon an Australian amusing himself with a large monkey which was wearing a dinky pair of pants and an Australian slouch hat. It was only when Bo-co turned round and showed his hairy back that we were certain who was who but looks, colour and nationality carry little weight out here so long as you can reach the firing Line, even if you can only crawl. Our well, eight feet in diameter, is now five feet deep. We have to erect a tripod with three two-inch steel pipes. A pulley at the apex is attached and the job of hoisting this awkward contraption is accomplished, under the supervision of the Engineer, in a matter of seconds.

Digging was resumed but there was no sign of water when we had a break for tea. Sitting around the top of the dry well, we watched a Taube aircraft very high in the sky. It had dropped several bombs which we heard falling. They didn't make much impression – a dull thud and a shower of earth and stones. One bomb fell fairly near and, in our rush into the well, we brought down the tripod. Whatever fell from the aircraft didn't appear to explode but made a hole about six feet deep, deeper than our well. We dug around for some time but couldn't locate a bomb.

We arrived back at our dump at about six in the evening and were immediately warned to be in the firing line at eight. There was time for a cup of tea – at least we made time – and then went back to the line to begin a bombing sap that was urgently needed. We went underneath the parapet with very little effort and straight into a shell-hole, which made less digging for us. The lads in the line filled the sandbags and built the walls through the shell-hole. We then had a dump close at hand to hide the excavated earth. It had to be hidden, because the moisture to it gave it a darker colour. Normally we would have thrown the earth out on both sides of the trench to give additional cover but the Turks would have been able to observe its length and direction. To avoid this we pushed out and the infantry followed on making the sap the required depth in comparative safety.

Saturday, July 17th

We worked all through the night and at dawn had made satisfactory progress. The bombing sap was almost complete when the Turks attacked the sector. All available men were on the fire step. The Turks came forward in waves but none reached our line. It was they who were burying their faces in the prickly scrub now as I had had to do so many times.

The attack, though menacing for a time, faded out, Our forward trench had already paid for the effort put into its construction. The bomber chaps had been able to throw their deadly jam tins and scatter the oncoming enemy, the troops in the line doing the rest.

After a little tidying up we were withdrawn to our base.

Sunday, July 18th

Today we do not have any particular job to do. We are in the frontline, a little further to the right, and helping to make the trench look a bit respectable. Burying the dead takes up most of the time as there are many to bury.

Monday, July 19th

We remained at our base until late in the afternoon, having a half-day off for a change. We did not reach the firing line until early evening. The Hood Battalion was holding this part and the Turks had established a barricade much too close for our liking. During the night a company of Hoods rushed the barricade and, after considerable fighting, managed to secure themselves to it, thereby adding another forty yards or so to our foothold on the Peninsula. This will be described in the official communique as a 'minor operation'. Minor be damned; though small in area, it was a great fight and very costly to both sides. Helping to consolidate the newly-won ground took up most of our stay in the line but we found time to dig a few holes about a foot deep in the bottom of the trench. With a bit of luck about an inch of water might trickle in during the course of the day, to be shared by all present – however many. A day's wait for a cupful of water!

Tuesday, July 20th

Today we began to sink a well on 'X' Beach. This was really comical; only a matter of hours ago we were sucking stones to quench our terrible thirsts and today we are actually only a few yards from the water's edge with as much water as we want – a bit salty but not nearly so salty as urine.

Fancy sinking a well here, but to our astonishment we soon had the most successful well on the Peninsula – pure, lovely, refreshingly cool water – gallons and gallons of it. How we wished we would carry the lot to the front Line and give those poor, half-baked, nearly savage ghosts a treat. As we continued to dig we wasted gallons, throwing out more water than earth. We worked all the time up to our knees in it but the water on our cheeks was not all coming from the splashes we were making with our shovels. We were grieved to see such waste but it was unavoidable as we must sink deeper and deeper to ensure a regular supply. If we could have got just a little to those parched throats on the front fine it would have been appreciated more than all the wealth in the world. Money is of no value out here; man is as good as his master. Rich or poor, the chances of survival are equal and the betting is one-hundred-to-one you don't. Those that are alive at the moment are not fully conscious of the fact. They are mechanical ghosts; all the fighting men are ghosts – officers and men alike. There is, though, that great comradeship, ever-changing but always great. Each day – sometimes each hour – someone joins the phantom army, the army of the dead, and those that are left walk about in a dream wondering how long they will be spared.

Wednesday, July 21st

Further progress was made with our well. The inrush of water was so great that we could not dig any deeper. We had got over the joke and the more water we wasted, the more painful it became. We rigged up a huge canvas container and the lads queued to fill their bottles. It was a lovely sight with no restrictions whatever, just 'Help yourselves, lads'.

The horses and mules – hundreds of them – were not forgotten. We had another container for them, too, to enjoy a drink.

I was not sorry when we had orders to move up the coast to Gully Ravine. Some distance up the ravine we began another well. There was about two feet of sandy soil and then solid rock. It was so dry that we had to walk over a mile to obtain sufficient water to enable us to drill the holes in readiness for blasting. Day after day we blasted in more ways than one but, having reached a depth of thirty-four feet without even a slight trace of dampness, we gave it up as hopeless. Imagine our surprise when the Engineer-in-charge marked out a spot for another well only a few feet from the white elephant. He said we should have struck water thereabouts and was certain we would be successful with this new well. Strange to say, we found traces of dampness almost at once and at four feet had to bale water all the time to get on with the sinking. At six feet the inrush was so hampering our digging that we decided to cut a trench between the two wells so that the water could run into the first one close by. At ten feet we had to abandon all further sinking as we had a supply well and a thirty-four-foot deep container. Our only regret was that it was some distance from the line.

We sank several more wells but were never quite so successful as we had been with this one in the gully and the one on 'X' Beach.

CHAPTER NINE

AUGUST

Sunday, August 1st

We began cutting saps from the front line – short trenches towards the Turkish front line which were intended to be used as bombing posts. In some cases they were joined with similar saps and in effect we advanced our firing line without exposing the troops to the murderous fire of the enemy. Quite a lot of nasty bends were straightened out by this method.

Friday, August 6th

All work on the line has been suspended for the time being and we have been held in readiness to proceed up the line at a moment's notice. At 2.30 pm. a terrific bombardment was commenced by our artillery on the left flank, assisted by two Monitors – one sending over fourteen-inch shells and the other nine-inch shells. Just like old times; the left flank was advancing. The returning wounded said they had captured two lines of, trenches but had lost a lot of men. This was not hard to believe, judging by the number of wounded coming back.

Saturday, August 7th

A repetition of yesterday – this time it was the centre who were advancing.

According to a wounded man, they had taken their objective – two lines – without much trouble but had been ordered to capture another trench about forty yards further on as well. It was in this last forty yards that they had met extremely severe opposition, so much so that they had been forced to retire to their original objective, the second trench.

The Turks had then counter-attacked and forced them to retire still further to the first of the captured trenches. Here they had remained for about half-an-hour whilst the artillery bombarded the Turks and they then advanced and recaptured the second trench. After a while the Turks counter-attacked repeatedly but were cut to pieces by the artillery.

Sunday, August 8th

We resumed our work of pushing saps forward from the front Line; this had been suspended because of the move forward during the last two days. Now we have a new line and bombing saps are urgently needed.

Today we are working on the left flank and have made considerable progress. We have had plenty of help from the infantry holding the line. Each day we are in a different part of the line, moving to the main from left to right By moving about the line as we do, I can see the real cost of the few yards of useless ground wrested from the Turks on the 6th and 7th. It is fatal to show one's head above the trench even for a fraction of a second but, by the aid of a periscope, I can see the dead lying everywhere. Out in front of the firing line and in between the lines the scene is the same – Turks as well as our own lads lying rotting to the sun. The stench is nauseating and the scene appalling.

Monday, August 16th

At 4 am the Highland Light Infantry captured a bombing post that was much too near them to be comfortable. It was a little to our right, but once the firing started it spread along the whole of the centre positions – shelling, bombing, rifle and machine-gun fire. Instead of digging we were on the fire step until well after dawn. Once a soldier, always a soldier, they say – it's true with us.

Friday, August 20th

Before leaving base for the line, we were told that there was going to be a bit of a sing-song to the evening by No. 2 Field Company, Divisional Engineers to the Ambulance Lines and we were not to be late. The last time (July 6th) we joined the Engineers for a sing-song I had certainly enjoyed it and the mug of cocoa that went with it. Tonight, we just managed to arrive in time as we had several odd jobs to do to the line before we were able to get away.

The evening was a great success and, as it was drawing to a close, I began making enquiries about our next get-together. To my dismay I was told there wouldn't be another.

'Those of you mining chaps that are left are to be transferred to a newly-formed 8th Army Corps Mining Company, with headquarters at Pink Farm,' we were told. 'You can report there tomorrow morning.'

I had enjoyed my stay with the Engineers – they had always been very nice to us.

Saturday, August 21st

We reported at Pink Farm as instructed and, after two hours' waiting, were sent off to establish an advanced base in the support line just to the rear of the vineyard. Our job was to make funk-holes for the men in the support trenches. A rather special dug-out was made in the First Australian Line which ran from the Fir Tree Wood to the Krithia Nullah. We went down about fifteen feet and dug a cave-like hole with a domed roof. I did not like it; it was a trap as no timber was available and a shell anywhere near it would certainly destroy it, with no escape for anyone.

Monday, August 23rd

Today we began sapping in earnest from the front line to a sector known as French Gully. Working in pairs, we did shifts of four hours on and four hours off. The first ten yards or so was an open sap towards the Turkish front Line; thence onwards we went below the surface to roughly three feet and a party of infantrymen were detailed to work for us by clearing away the earth in sandbags.

After about an hour's tunnelling we had just managed to secure the roof with timber when the Turks attacked the sap. The first bomb to fall into it blew my pal to pieces. A few moments previously we had been saying how lucky we were to be below ground and away from the flying splinters. He had been on his way to the trench to bring some more timber when the bomb fell on him.

The Turks got quite close but none entered the sap. The infantry saw to that they are great lads. After the raid, I worked on alone until my relief arrived. Work went on through-out the day and night and, after three days, we completed our task. We had an underground trench stretching some distance and its purpose was to establish a listening post to 'No-man's-land'. In the event of a further attack by our men it would enable them to get reinforcements and further supplies to then-new positions without exposing, themselves over the open ground. The infantrymen liked it very much as it gave them additional cover, not only from the bombs but from the scorching sun during the long day.

Friday, August 27th

We have been on the move again, from the vineyard to the centre to East Anglia Gully on the left. We established a base in the gully and went into the firing Line occupied by the Manchesters of the Forty-second Division. Here we commenced mining in earnest, driving an inclining shaft four feet, two inches high and two feet, two inches wide, from the firing line, to a depth of twenty-eight feet. We dug several of these shafts about twenty yards apart and, at about twenty feet below, we connected them up, thus making an underground trench beneath 'No-man's-land' so that we could hear and destroy any subsequent mining by the Turks without damaging our own line.

CHAPTER TEN

SEPTEMBER

Thursday, September 2nd

For several days now I have had a severe pain round my waist. Today a rash has broken out and the pain is excruciating. Huge blisters resembling raspberries are driving me frantic. I could not even bear my trousers touching me so I took them off and reported to the officer in charge, excusing my undress, which apparently amused him – not the nakedness but my apology for it. He instructed me to report sick at the hospital on the cliffs.

Upon arrival at the scores of tents on the cliff top I was taken, still in my birthday suit, before the doctor. He ordered a bath and a corporal of the RAMC was my nurse. In a matter of minutes he produced an iron affair partially filled with warm water. Even in a sitting position, the water did not cover my raspberries but the corporal and I were having a grand time splashing about with the warm disinfected water. Mother's good boy was having his bath, but the merriment did not last. Without the slightest warning there was a terrific crash and away went the tent and, with it, my nurse. The shell had fallen some distance away and I couldn't see any casualties. I did observe the shape of the corporal trying to extricate himself from underneath the shapeless mass of canvas that had been our tent I left my bathtub and assisted him in unravelling himself. He was unhurt and we began the business of the bath all over again as if nothing had happened; it was an open-air bath this time. However, it was completed to the corporal's satisfaction.

While we were looking for my elusive trousers, another shell landed in another part of the hospital and there were cries for help from several places. Off went the corporal, on his job of alleviating suffering, leaving me still naked and looking for my trousers. I soon found a fine pair of officer's shorts, and with them under my arm I reported back to Headquarters at Pink Farm where I was promptly ordered back to the hospital.

It was quite dark when I arrived back at the cliff top and I wanted it that way in case there was someone looking for his lost shorts. I spent quite a time looking for my corporal so that I could explain where I had been and also why. He was in no way surprised to see me.

'I knew you would turn up again' he said, 'and I would recognise your "Uniform" anywhere. You must have another bath at once.'

It was while I was partially immersed in carbolic that I told him the taleof my new shorts. 'There was I standing naked and feeling very sorry for myself when a gust of wind blew them literally at my feet.'

'You were carrying your trousers when you arrived and it is only right you should leave with some,' he said. 'Do the new ones fit you?'

'I don't know. I have not tried them on yet. My waist is too sore and your carbolic is driving me mad.'

'Let me know it they fit as soon as you can and, if they don't, I will get you some that will. We cannot have you going back to the firing line naked. If the Turks see you they will think we are all mad, though perhaps we are.'

Tuesday, September 7th

My raspberries have faded almost overnight. My shorts fit perfectly and I have been discharged from hospital.

I reported to Pink Farm and, after about an hour, joined my party and proceeded up the line on the left of the Gully. There was a lot of mining activity in this sector. We had several shafts almost completed and we were to join them up at a depth of about twenty feet. When our spell of duty was over we returned to our advanced base on the right of the Gully in a spot known as Geoghegan's Bluff.

Friday, September 10th

Whilst working in one of the shafts we heard the Turks digging and we estimated their distance to be about fifteen feet away. The sound was very faint but was unmistakably digging. We reported this at once to the captain in charge, who was at our headquarters at Pink Farm. He did not bother to come at once but came the following afternoon. As soon as he entered the gallery the digging, which had gone on without ceasing all the morning, stopped. He remained down below for a little while without hearing any digging but, almost as soon as he left, it was resumed. It seemed as though the Turks were actually watching his movements.

As the days passed, the digging continued, hourly becoming appreciably nearer, but whenever our officer came below it stopped at once. An instruction was issued to the effect that no mine was to be exploded until the Turks were within three feet of us. This may seem to be extremely risky – well it is risky, but the business of war is risky and we miners could judge the Turks' whereabouts almost to an inch by the sound of his digging. The trenches out here are so close to each other that we have to wait until the last moment before doing any blasting. Furthermore, we have to be exact in our calculations, not only of distance but of the amount of explosive to be used, as otherwise we would blow up our own firing line as well as the Turks'. It is not a pleasant task to keep on digging towards the enemy, when you are so near. Every time he stops we do also and until one of us resumes digging, we do not know whether he is making his mine ready to blow us sky high. Of course, he is in the same predicament as he must also hear us digging.

Tuesday, September 14th

In the early afternoon we were within the limit so we asked for and received permission to spring our mine. We had made a recess in which were laid three 10 lb. tins of Ammonal. The sandbags that would normally have been carried away were left for us to use as tamping. The detonators had been placed in one of the tins and the wires were carefully wrapped around one of the sandbags so that there would be no danger of pulling them from the tin during the tamping. Dozens and dozens of sandbags had to be carefully packed to ensure that the least resistance would be upwards; otherwise the force of the explosion would simply blow them away and we would completely destroy our own gallery and do absolutely no damage to the Turkish firing line some twenty-eight feet above.

We normally allowed ourselves fifteen minutes for this preparation but as we felt the urgency, called for a speed-up. We were ready in a little over ten minutes. At almost exactly 3 pm the men in the line were warned that we were going to blast and down went the plunger. With a terrific bang, up went the mine and, with it, the Turkish front line. Our line trembled; huge chunks of earth fell everywhere from the cloud of dust – that shrouded the entire scene.

So for my part ended four very trying days of which every moment had been a nightmare.

After a few minutes we were able to re-enter our own mine-shaft. It had suffered a little from the blast but now the imminent danger had passed, we began clearing up and soon had the place tidy again. The tamping had to be removed and we were pleased it had withstood the force of the explosion. As we neared the seat of the explosion we found the roof to be in a bad state and had to use more timber than usual. This slowed our progress and our reliefs arrived before we had cleared the tamping, but they were able to finish the job.

Wednesday, September 15th

Coming on duty in the afternoon a little later than usual and with a couple of extra men, we were able to carry on our normal work. The lads we relieved had made a good job of the clearing up and had made the roof reasonably safe. They had begun to go forward and we continued in that direction. We would soon need the working party who were waiting in the shade at the entrance.

Our conversation was on the usual topic – food. What would we have for supper? The chaps we relieved would be going to the beach for the rations and one of them casually mentioned he had heard a rumour that someone had actually seen a tin of butter. We felt sorry for him; the sun had obviously caught him – but in our hearts we clung to the faint hope that he might be right after all. Anyway, the parting shot was 'Don't forget the butter'.

A glance at my watch told me it was almost 5 pm. and my thoughts wandered but still on the subject of food. The ration party would be arriving at the beach about now; they would have a swim first.

Then I must have dozed. I seemed to visualise myself diving in off the end of the pier and groping for a tin of condensed milk 'accidentally' placed there whilst unloading boxes from the barges. It was extremely dark and I could not understand this as it is usually quite light and a broken box lying on the sea-bed does not normally present any difficulty at all. Maybe I was underneath a barge alongside the pier. I was very confused as there were no barges in sight when I dived in. There couldn't have been, otherwise I could not have entered the water from the end of the pier. I had completely lost the run of things but somehow felt extremely happy. I was in a world of my own – a world of complete silence – yet I did not feel alone. I wandered about, though not aimlessly. I knew where I wanted to go but somehow could not quite get on the right road.

It was still very dark but in the distance there appeared to be a faint glow. It was as though I was waiting for the sun to rise over a very distant horizon and an unseen hand was leading me over the rough ground towards the still distant glow. I could feel the grip of my guide, but couldn't see who it was.

Day after day we stumbled on; at least I stumbled but my guide seemed to be very sure-footed. He knew the way and never faltered – over mountains and down valleys – with the light still in the distance as a soft, encouraging glow. As we climbed out of a huge crater, the soft glow became a brilliant light over the top of the mountain; yet all around me was very dark. But I knew now that I was on the right road and hastened to the top from where I could see green fields and gentle wooded slopes leading down to the river which, as a boy, I had many times crossed by way of the slippery stepping-stones just beneath the surface of the fast-flowing water. We used to take off our boots and stockings, hang them over our necks and cross in our bare feet.

I can remember the time when Billy Ellis and I were crossing. His laces broke and in trying to grab at his falling shoes, he fell in, dragging me with him. We searched for nearly a mile down the rock-strewn river for one of Billy's shoes but did not find it and poor Billy had to walk the couple of miles home to a good hiding, in his bare feet. I would not have to cross the river to reach my destination, one of the tiny hamlets that had grown up around the mine-shafts that bored deep down into the rocky hillside, each with its own pyramid-shaped slag heap to mar the lovely countryside.

The way ahead seemed easy and, as I began my descent, I felt the grip of my guide's hand gradually loosening until it was no longer discernible but I was still not alone. I was never alone, yet I could not see my guide.

On and on down the hillside until I reached my own particular slag-heap with the customary wisp of smoke rising from its top, then across the cricket field to the garden with the fence made of railway sleepers. The path to my home had been newly covered with the red ash from the burning slag-heap. It was as it a red carpet had been laid for my visit.

My mother was sitting under the lilac tree which shaded the door. A tall woman dressed in black was in earnest conversation with her. I think she was trying to console Mother, who was obviously grieved. For the first time during my long journey I felt uncertain as to what to do. As I stood there, bewildered, she rose from her seat and, with tears streaming down her cheeks, came towards me with arms outstretched saying: I'm glad you are safe, Joe. Be a man, always be the man you are.'

We walked arm-in-arm back to her chair and as she sat down the weight of years left her face; she was young again with a charming smile covering her sweet, beautiful face – the face of an angel.

When the time came for me to take my leave I could not turn my back on such loveliness, such contentment. I moved backwards very slowly, waving to her as I did when I left home in October nearly a year ago. I knew she could not see me now but I kept on waving just the same until my hands came into contact with yet another hand. Unlike the hand of my guide, it was icy cold and rough...

It was the hand of my mate, Alec. He told me that we had been blown up.

I was fully awake now but could not for the life of me understand how the Turks had managed to spring their mine so soon. Only yesterday we had blown them sky-high from this very spot. Nor could I understand why I could see Alec. The brilliant light of a moment ago had gone and darkness had returned, yet I had a clear picture of Alec leaning over me, a trickle of blood from his nose dripping on my face. As I moved my head aside to avoid it, the picture of Alec faded away. I used my hand to wipe my face, but to no avail, as my nose was also bleeding.

Alec and I groped about in the dark, looking for our candles and matches. We found neither so decided to explore the gallery to ascertain where the explosion had occurred. The level part was reasonably clear. Several minor falls of roof had taken place but we had no difficulty in climbing over these obstructions to reach the rising part. From here we should have been able to see daylight, but we couldn't.

We knew now that we were entombed but the gallery was still open. We groped our way up the rising gallery and at once realised we should not be able to go much further. Everywhere was broken up. Timber – not broken but dislodged – prevented any further movement up the slope and we did not know if this blockage was the seat of the explosion or only another fall. We tugged at the timber until we got it free. Quite a lot of earth came away with it which told us we had no more gallery left and our only hope of survival would be to claw our way upwards through the broken earth, knowing full well that if it was too loose it would suffocate us. We estimated that we were at least twenty-five feet below the surface because a week ago we had begun to connect up the shafts at a depth of twenty feet The activities of the Turks had prevented us from continuing with this connecting gallery and we had then concentrated on stopping his progress towards us.

We were somewhere below that point and decided that if we endeavoured to burrow slantwise, making steps as we went, we would have further to go but would be able to get rid of some of the earth and, at the same time, have more room for air.

I began to burrow, with Alec behind me heaving the lumps of clay down the eight feet or so of the sloping gallery. We changed over repeatedly and, as time passed, found it increasingly difficult to clear the earth away. The burrow behind us had closed in and the roof kept caving in. We were unable to extricate ourselves from the earth we had clawed away and the constant falling of the roof altered our direction.

We burrowed where the earth was loose, clawing side by side now, with only our arms free. Inching our way upwards, we clawed with our hands and pushed with our legs to keep us moving. We had very little room but the air seemed better. The earth felt more lumpy and we found it difficult to move. Lumps of earth were wedged between us and were most uncomfortable.

Twisting and turning in an effort to free my legs, I fancied I saw daylight for a fraction of a second. Alec did not see it, but believed me. With new hope we struggled on; our time was running out and we both knew it. Again and again we were completely buried but, in time, managed to clear ourselves. After one fall of earth I could feel what I believed to be clothing. It certainly was not earth – and I was violently sick.

Alec was delighted though; in his superhuman effort to free his legs so that he might also feel the body, he brought down more earth and shouted that he, too, had seen daylight. This time I did not see it – I was too sick and my eyes were closed, but as I had seen daylight some time ago, I was satisfied that we were near the surface. If only we could both see daylight at the same time. This body we could feel must have been in the line; if only we could manage a few more feet!

With renewed strength we clawed but the daylight – if it was daylight – remained out of sight.

We had burrowed a long way and the hope of a while ago had long since gone. I think we slept from exhaustion. We had lost all sense of time and it seemed that we had been entombed all our lives.

I was awakened by Alec shouting that he could see daylight again. The air was certainly fresher. I had lots of energy now and, after another fall of earth, we had our heads above the Surface. My arms were pinned with the rest of my body and the glare of the light, even though it was almost dark, compelled me to keep my eyes closed. I did have a glance at Alec who was a grinning minstrel. He said I looked like Jem Mace.

Strangely enough, neither of us made any attempt to free ourselves. We were satisfied to have our heads above ground. We were on the Turkish side of a huge crater, about five feet below the rim. There was no sign of any trench – nothing but lumps of brown clay.

After a while we managed to free our arms. We called out quietly but got no response. We called again, a little louder this time. We fancied we could see an occasional movement just over the rim on our side so we called yet again and several bayonets appeared. We knew then that our calls had been heard. After what seemed ages, a head very slowly appeared above the rim and, although it looked directly at us, gave no sign of recognition.

'You belong to the 42nd Division; we are sappers. We are half-buried – get some shovels and dig us out,' we said.

The head sank out of sight and remained hidden from view. It would be dark in half-an-hour or even less so we must free ourselves. We set about the task but our strength had gone. Our fingers were so sore and bleeding that we made little head-way. We had to struggle to keep awake, going through the movements automatically with our eyes closed.

Alec was saying something I could not understand. I forced my eyes open so that I could see what he wanted me to do. It was very dark and all that I could see was a strange, hard, grimy face almost touching mine. It was Old Nick himself and the breath from the demon's nostrils seemed to burn my cheeks. In fear I quickly closed my eyes but a heavy slap on my face made me lash out with my fists. When I made contact I opened my eyes. Old Nick had gone and I was almost free.

Lying beside Alec and me were two men. 'You must be the Manchesters,' I said.

'That's reet, lad,' came the reply.

A few hefty pulls and Alec and I were crawling up the rim of the crater, helped by the two men. Seconds later we were back in the front line – or what was left of it. The Turkish mine had exploded just short of our line and completely filled it. It was thought that about thirty of the Manchesters had been buried.

One of our mine-shafts known as 'Four Hole Post' could not be located; there had been four of our sappers in it at the time. The infantry holding the line had almost completed the re-digging of the trench and a party of sappers had begun to dig a new No. 1 Gallery. They were waiting for Alec and me.

Evidently, when they had been told that two of their pals were out in front they had to be forcibly restrained from coming to us. They made no attempt to conceal their pleasure at seeing us again but no one mentioned the explosion. I was beginning to think it was only a dream; it seemed so long ago.

I found it difficult to follow the conversation. Every now and again I would catch a word but could not connect it with the previous word and I asked. 'Why all the Whispering?' Alec was poking his ear with his finger and I did the same. It was painful and I felt my fingers bleeding again, but I could now hear the conversation much more clearly. I still could not understand what they were saying, though. Someone said: 'Let the poor devils sleep', and, hearing the mention of devils, I closed my eyes tightly.

When I awoke it was daylight Alec was still asleep but soon opened his eyes when he, like me, was offered a mug of tea.

Very much refreshed by the sleep and the lovely cup of tea, we made our way to the new No. 1 sap to thank the sappers for their help, only to find they had been relieved long ago. We had lost all sense of time. We then began looking for the two Manchesters who had brought us back to the line. We very much wanted to thank them and I to apologise for lashing out at them. An officer to whom I explained my mission thanked me for my concern and said he would convey our message when he found the men.

'Stop worrying and go back to your base and finish that sleep,' he said. So it was you, I thought, that I had heard saying 'Let the poor devils sleep'.

'You both looked as it you needed a good sleep,' he continued. 'How do you feel now?'

'Fine, sir, thank you, and please thank those two men of yours. We are most grateful.'

Friday, September 17th

In the early morning we made our way back and, upon arrival at Geogheghan's Bluff, had a long talk with the lieutenant in charge. He was most interested in our escape. He said he had been told of our safety in the early hours of the morning but when he reached the line we were fast asleep. He was deeply concerned when we told him that No. 1 sap was open from the 'face' to a point about eight feet up the slope.

'The Turks might hole it,' he said, 'and if they did they could destroy the whole of our system. We must get there before they do. I must go to the line at once.' After ordering us to rest, he left

When we were fully rested we began to move about. We ached all over but our eyes had by now got used to the glare of the sun after thirty-six hours of total darkness – thirty-one of them entombed.

It seemed years since I had seen the sea. When, in the late afternoon, the ration party set off for the beach. Alec and I joined them. We felt the walk and the company would help us to get back to normal routine.

The Turks shelled the Gully as we made our way down and we were forced to take cover many times from the shrapnel bursting overhead. We arrived safely, though, and were all soon splashing about in the sea like a group of school boys. How I needed that wash. The cuts on my face and body hurt but they were nothing compared with the excruciating pain of my finger tips, which bled all the time I was in the sea. By the time I was dressed, though, the smarting and the bleeding had almost ceased. My fingernails were all broken so I told Alec I was going to the First Aid Post at the foot of the cliff to have them trimmed up a bit and he came along with me as his were in a similar state.

The medical orderly, a nice chap, trimmed our nails and painted our fingers with a concoction that looked like yellow iodine which made them smart like the very devil. He then bandaged our fingers and told us we must report to the hospital at once. We agreed to do this and thanked him for his services. As we left I could see what was in Alec's mind but, as his fingers were in a much worse state than mine, I suggested that he lead the way and this he did, though in the opposite direction to the hospital.

Our party had collected the rations and were waiting for us. We offered to carry something but they only laughed at us. With our black faces and white 'gloves' all we needed were straw hats.

Back at our advanced base, we reported for duty. The lieutenant said he was short of men but we could have a few days off if we wanted them. 'You have both had a very nasty experience. We had given you up; how on earth you managed to get out of that lot I just cannot understand and never shall,' he said.

Saturday, September 18th

Alec and I relieved the men down in No. 3 sap at 4 am The Turks could be heard digging in several places but they were quite a long way off and there was nothing to worry about for a day or two. Both Alec and I found it difficult to dig but we soon made a showing and when our reliefs came at 8 o'clock we, and they, were satisfied with the work. After the usual chat we left, to return at midday.

The Turkish digging was appreciably nearer but still not near enough to worry about We had just got settled in nicely when the whole place trembled and out went the candles. The working party was spaced along the whole gallery. Matches were struck and candles re-lighted but there was no apparent damage, I ordered the working party out and Alec and I followed after making a thorough inspection of the gallery.

Upon reaching the firing line we were directed to No. 1 Sap which the Turks had another crack at, as on the 15th, they had aimed short and there was very little damage to the gallery and no casualties. The troops were 'standing to' so we had to manage without the working party. The firing had eased by now; each time the Turk springs a mine he commences rapid firing. We went below and spent some time listening to his digging; we could now hear him in three different places.

Sunday, September 19th

Coming on duty at 4 am, we were told that the Turkish digging on the left was now fairly close. We all listened and decided that we must prepare to blast. We held on to the filled sandbags as we should need them soon. The chaps going off for four hours reported the state of affairs to the lieutenant. It was about 7 am. when he came down to the gallery and, having heard the digging, decided to blast at once as the Turks were by now well within the three-foot margin.

We were all ready and had been for some time. The Turk's position was such that if we made the usual recess to plant our explosive, we should hole into his gallery or he would fall through into our recess. Extra tamping was needed and the filled sandbags had to be brought back down the slope, much to the disgust of the Manchester lads.

'Make tha mind up, lad. Dust tha want the muk in or oot?'

It was good-tempered joking; if the truth were known, they were even more anxious than we – it that was possible – to blow the blighter sky high.

We took a little longer than usual to get the mine ready because of the extra tamping needed to preserve our own gallery. The seat of the explosion was to be in the gallery instead of in the normal recess.

After about twenty minutes all was ready, the men in the line 'stood to', the lieutenant pressed the plunger down and up went the Turkish front line and, with it, an awful lot of worry.

Unfortunately several of our troops were hurt by the falling lumps of clay, the trenches being so close at this point that it was impossible to avoid this. The usual rapid firing broke out which spread right across to the extreme left at Fusilier Bluff. The firing went on until midday, both artilleries joining in.

Monday, September 20th

Clearing up the gallery took up most of the morning. We could still hear the Turks digging. It was not continuous – very faint and quite a long way off. We felt safe for a few days. When our reliefs arrived, we reported this digging and, having satisfied ourselves that there was no immediate danger, took our leave.

We had only gone a few paces when there was an explosion. There was no damage to speak of and no one hurt. We all assembled in the firing line and the sappers from Nos. 1 and 2 saps were relieved to find that we from No. 3 were safe.

It was agreed that an attempt had been made again on No. 3 sap. This was getting far too regular and was decidedly unhealthy. We wasted over an hour trying to figure out this Chinese puzzle, all making various suggestions, but in the end coming no nearer the solution than we were at the beginning. There was general agreement that the Turk overcharges his mines. He has had several cracks at our galleries but, compared with the amount of work he has obviously put in, he has not done very much damage to them, yet he has killed, wounded and buried quite a lot of men in our firing line. On the 15th he had completely filled-in a whole section, destroying two of our galleries.

I cannot understand how he is able to retaliate. We have blown him sky-high several times, yet he is able to hit back. In the main his mines are short but on the last occasions he has passed our galleries. Thank God he was short again today.

We stayed to help our reliefs tidy up the mess. Quite a lot of extra timber had to be used as the gallery was badly shaken and in places in danger of collapse.

Satisfied that things were under control, we took our leave for the second time and made our way back to the base, very satisfied that now the Turk had let off his firecracker we could safely assume that we should have a couple of days free from blasting.

What a relief; two whole days without anything to worry about except bullets, shells, bombs and, maybe, a frontal day or night attack. We had had similar thoughts this morning but the Turk had foxed us.

Tuesday, September 21st

It was almost midnight and I was clearing the mess in No. 3 sap. The previous shift had moved most of our tamping. My pick struck a piece of sacking – a strange find twenty-eight feet below the surface; these two explosions must have turned the world upside down. It was not something of ours, I was sure. The earth was very loose, as we expected it to be, and I kept on digging until I came across an almost complete sandbag. After this find I used my hands to clear away the earth and revealed many others. It was evident that we had reached the Turkish gallery and these sandbags were his tamping. They were in position so we must be sitting on the Turk's mine – not a pleasant thought.

We sent a message to Headquarters and awaited the lieutenant, who arrived out of breath. There were more questions, answers and measurements.

'Yes, that's about right; five feet eight inches exactly from the beginning of our own tamping, plus two feet for our mine and another two feet for his mine.'

'We seem to have won by a short head,' remarked the lieutenant. There's not much more than a foot between us but we are all right this side of the Turk's tamping. If his gallery has stood the shock as well as ours then he may be removing his tamping and, as we are helping him at this end, we shall soon be shaking hands with him. He cannot be more than five feet away. Again, if he is using his hands to remove the sandbags, we shall not hear him.

Wednesday, September 22nd

We were due to be relieved at 6 am., but at 5.30 I unearthed some copper wire similar to ordinary telegraph wire. It was quite new and I had some difficulty in cutting it My once razor-sharp jack-knife was not quite so sharp, but had given me good service. Without it, Alec and I would still be in No. 1 sap.

The officer in charge of the firing line was immediately told of my find. He at once came to see me and took the piece of wire I had cut out. He said he had burst all his trouser buttons on the way down and, apart from being a keepsake, the wire would have to substitute for the buttons.

Instead of our reliefs arriving at 6 am, the lieutenant came alone. He said it would be advisable for us to finish the job and instructed us to follow the wire very cautiously. He would arrange for us to be relieved at noon if we had not completed the task by then.

During the morning we were visited by a continuous stream of officers, including several French Staff Officers. Each party had to be told the history of the captured gallery and each had to have a piece of wire to take away. We were only just able to unearth enough wire to satisfy the demands of the next batch of visitors.

At 9.30 am the order came down that all men must be in the firing line at once so out we came, to be told that there was to be a show at Fusilier Bluff on the extreme left. We were most interested as we had worked in that sector for a considerable time. We had begun, with the help of the infantry, to dig a wide trench from the firing line towards the cliff-top away from the Turks. We then made a fairly deep gallery in the same direction and, much to their annoyance, the infantry had to fill the open trench they had laboriously dug with the earth we excavated from the gallery. We humoured them by saying we were actually making very roomy, deep dug-outs for them and must hide the damp earth; otherwise the Turks would be aware of their exact location. The damp excavated earth would not be noticed in a newly dug trench, as trenches 'were being dug all the time.'

The gallery led towards the cliffs and eventually holed in a lovely spot – a sheer drop into the sea almost in the middle of a small bay.

So had ended the first phase. The next was to mine towards' the Turks. We went down more steeply than usual to the required depth. The earth was very suitable for mining in this area and we made good progress, soon reaching our forward limit The several galleries were then connected, giving us an advanced underground trench some thirty feet underneath the Turkish firing line.

The next operation was to push forward to certain strong-points beyond the Turk's front line. My particular objective was a redoubt beyond his second line, a mass of machine-gun posts that not only protected his right flank but dominated the whole area. By getting rid of the earth via the gallery to the cliffs we were able to honeycomb the whole area unmolested.

I, with others, was withdrawn to the other side of the gully, but many sappers remained to continue the project.

It was their show we were now watching. Our infantrymen on the left had begun rapid firing, a ruse to bring the Turks into their firing line in readiness for an imminent attack. As our fire lessened, that of the Turks increased and spread to our side of the gully. The sharp crack of the rifles, the rat-a-tat of the machine-guns, the deep thud of the shells and the fantastic patterns of the shrapnel bursts above the blue haze were really awesome to us, the onlookers. There was then a tremendous boom, followed by a slowly rising dome of black smoke which seemed reluctant to disperse; for some minutes it obscured the whole area.

Except for an occasional rifle-crack, the firing had now ceased and all was deadly quiet The 610 pounds of Ammonal had done its devastating job. I was pleased to be able to witness the final act as I had been part of the play, but now the show was over and the final curtain run down, I felt very uneasy as I went back into the captured Turkish gallery; it was so quiet.

Our reliefs had arrived in time for the show. Like us, they had worked quite a while in the galleries on Fusilier Bluff. They were now Instructed to work round the Turkish sandbags on the right. Two additional crews had arrived, making six men in all, one crew in the forward position, another starting a connecting gallery towards No. 2 sap and the third sapping in the opposite direction.

After our customary little chat, we left them to get on with their work and made our way back to base in the gully. We lost no time on the way as we had to be back in the gallery by 6 pm. On our arrival we were agreeably surprised to find tea all ready for us in honour of the historic event.

The capture of a Turkish gallery was an achievement worthy of note in this ding-dong struggle. A few of the sappers from Fusilier Bluff had come across to congratulate us and we in turn reciprocated. They had that morning given the Turks something to get on with.

We spent a pleasant afternoon swapping yarns, not all of them repeatable. At 5.30 pm. we left for our respective jobs, they to the Bluff and we six to our pet gallery – No. 3 – on the other side of the gully. We arrived at the appointed time, 6 pm., and found everything quite peaceful and going according to plan. No digging had been heard since we left.

With the usual 'Best of Luck' parting shot the relieved sappers left, but after five minutes or so, one of them returned to tell us. that an officer in the line had reported to him that one of his men had heard digging about twenty yards further along the line to the right. It was agreed that Alec and I should go and see the officer who was waiting at the entrance to the gallery. We found him and we then went to the spot indicated.

Alec and I crawled in opposite directions along the bottom of the trench, our ears almost touching the earth. In the next bay I could hear the sound of digging, so faintly that I could not define its direction. I called Alec and asked him to listen. After a minute or so he rose to his feet and said quite loudly, 'No... NO.' This was reassuring to the infantrymen holding the line. I could see the relief on their faces and tenseness had given way to slight smiles. I even forced myself to smile and felt ashamed of my deceit for I knew that when Alec had said 'No, no' it meant that he also had heard digging. We had had this arrangement for a long time. If either of us was asked to check the other's listening, 'no' meant no, but 'no, no' said loud enough for the men around to hear meant that we had both heard digging.

Addressing the officer I asked him if he would care to come with us and we would let him hear real digging down one of our galleries. He readily agreed and as soon as it was convenient we told him that the soldier had been correct. There was digging – we had both heard it and estimated it to be about fifteen feet away. It was too near our line for us to do anything. If we attempted to stop the Turks we would blow up our own trench. On the other hand, they could, and probably would, spring a mine and that would be the end of our firing line just the same. We would report the matter to Headquarters, and we knew the officer would also report it, but in the meantime he could come along and hear some real digging.

The officer thanked us for not alarming his men and for being so frank with him.

As we made our way towards No. 3 gallery he said he felt as if he was sitting on top of a volcano waiting for it to erupt. Almost as he spoke, that's just what happened. There was a sickening thud; the ground trembled and showers of earth came crashing down upon us, the resultant dust hindering our vision. A mine had gone up, but where? It was almost impossible to move along the trench.

Half-dazed, I remember the officer tousling my hair and saying: 'Must see to my men, laddie, but I will come back to you.'

As I watched him scramble over the uneven mounds that lay in the trench, I saw a poor chap rushing frantically along the parapet yelling and waving his arms. I called to him to come into the trench but he rushed towards the Turkish line and that was the last I saw of him.

The noise was by now deafening and shells and bullets were flying about everywhere. I was now fully conscious and rushed the few yards that separated me from No. 3 gallery but for the life of me I could not locate its entrance. I knew that the explosion must have been in this area. I knew also that my four pals and about a dozen of the working party I had left about a quarter of an hour ago had been in the gallery when the mine exploded.

After several trial digs Alec and I unearthed a piece of timber. A self-appointed working party were helping us. True to his word, the officer returned. 'You can have as many men as you require, laddie,' he said and began using a shovel as adeptly as the next man. The six sappers we had relieved, on hearing the explosion had come back and were working like slaves. There was more timber, more bodies and more bombs claiming their quota of dead and wounded. It was midnight before we gave up hope. No. 3 gallery had been blasted for the last time and now ceased to exist

Thursday, September 23rd

In the very early hours of the cool, sad morning, we eight sappers made our way down the gully mourning the loss of yet another four of our rapidly decreasing band. I cannot recall anyone speaking during the whole journey; we were stunned into silence.

The wily old Turk had us all guessing. Our first impression was that the sappers who were probing the captured gallery had set off the Turkish mine or that the Turks had placed another mine on their side of the tamping but now we knew the truth. The mine had been only a few feet from our firing line and it was painfully obvious that the Turks had had this gallery completed long before we began sapping in this sector.

How many more had he ready? We had repeatedly reported hearing digging close to our line; the infantry had also reported the fact. Alec and I had been brought out of the ill-fated gallery to listen to further digging only a matter of minutes before it was destroyed. The powers-that-be knew all this, yet nothing is being done. It is just a question of time and Johnnie Turk holds all the aces.

Breakfast time and no breakfast – just like the old days! Who was to blame this time? There was no grumbling, though, as the party who should have brought up the rations had, returned to the line and worked with us until after midnight trying to rescue our pals and, because of this, had missed the ration boat.

Several of us set off down the gully in the hope of finding something to eat. I, as usual, removed the 'Woodbine' packet from Tootsie's toes. Tootsie being a skeleton. I must have done this scores of times, in fact every time I passed this way the inevitable cigarette packet caught my eye. At first I looked upon it as a rotten type of joke but, as time went on, I considered it my duty to remove the offending packet, today especially. I would never know the nationality of Tootsie. Friend or enemy, he had been some mother's son, dying in his generosity for all that the name of his country stood for, hastily buried where he fell whilst cherishing the hope of a better world, trodden upon by countless feet that might by now have found their final resting place in the same soil.

It is only by the grace of God that I do not share his resting place and it is by that same grace that I am able to continue with my sordid mission. Tootsie's flesh has gone long ago and only the bones remain; if only they would decay and crumble into dust, how comforting it would be.

The sight of the sea banished all our worries and we splashed about like a lot of school-kids minus their complexions. We are old and worn, yet on our blackened skin there is a deathly pallor like a mask encasing every face and a vacant ghostly stare penetrates our bluff armour. Whilst we are conscious of, this we seldom notice it in the forward lines where all the fighting men are alike but down here on the beach we not only see it but feel it. Some of the pale faces have just arrived on the Peninsula but there are many that have been here long enough to take root, but still do not know where the trenches are. They are very well acquainted with the Quartermaster's Store. For every man in the line there appears to be about ten that are always out of it These fellows are those who, in later years, you will hear telling the willing listener how they won the Great War, how they went short of food and water. Maybe they did for half-an-hour but I doubt if their sacrifice lasted much longer. Very, very few men who win wars live long enough even to know the value of their contribution. They just fade away, as the old song says, and no one seems to care a tinker's damn.

After our dip in the briny we made our way up the gully to our base. The sappers had gone up to the line. They had had nothing to eat so we left at once, taking something for them. They had begun to sap from No. 2 gallery towards the ill-fated No. 3. They were about ten yards apart and a good start had been made. Several pairs of timbers were already in position. The earth was quite solid and because of this, after consultation with the other sappers, we decided to go forward without timber. We were working against time. If No. 3 gallery was open at the far end as was the case with No. 1 on the fifteenth, it could be that some of our pals might still be alive. The less earth we removed, the quicker, we would reach them. With this object in view, we simply burrowed a more or less round hole. There was not sufficient room to throw out the earth so the man doing the digging folded his arms round it and was dragged out clutching as much as he could hold between his arms. The man who dragged him out then took his place whilst he filled the sandbags where there was room to do so. He also set about enlarging the burrow and thereby lessening the drag. The working party dragged the filled sandbags away and helped in many other ways.

Friday, September 24th

The Turks made themselves a nuisance the whole day and, in consequence, the working party was called upon to remain in the firing line. We carried on as usual as there was no time to lose. During lulls, the men came down and cleared the sandbags. We were never really held up. We had, of course, further to drag the sapper clutching the earth but we had made progress.

On the arrival of our reliefs, we would go back for a rest and something to eat and drink, returning in four hours.

So it went on and we reckoned to reach No. 3 gallery sometime on sunday

Sunday, September 26th

This lovely Sunday morning saw Alec and me back in the rabbit hole at 6 am. The previous shift had made excellent progress. Almost at once Alec said he thought he could hear faint digging. We listened together for a short while but could hear nothing. A couple of hours later I thought I could hear digging again; again we listened together but with the same result. We were both certain that we had heard digging but as we did not hear it when we listened together, there was nothing we could do about it. In fact, even if we had heard it together there was precious little we could do.

The working party was due to be relieved at eleven o'clock and it was while this relief was taking place that Alec called out to me that he thought we were nearly through. I called back that he must be mistaken as we had at least ten feet to go yet.

'Never mind about ten feet I say we are almost through – it is very loose.'

I offered to take over the digging but he would not listen and kept slogging away like a madman.

'What did I tell you. I have struck timber.'

Soon he was confronted with a solid 'face' of wood. We were amazed as we had never timbered our galleries in this fashion. I sent an urgent note explaining the position to our Headquarters at Pink Farm, through the officer in charge of the line.

In the meantime we tried and tried to break through the wooden barrier, but to no avail. We were so anxious to get beyond it that we did not do the obvious thing for some little time, this being to dig upwards or downwards until we found the cross-member. Then, instead of pushing the barrier, edging it towards us. If the Turks' timber was similar to ours, an inch-and-a-half would be sufficient to allow, the cross-member to fall out of position. We could then force the upright forward into what we now knew by the sound to be an open gallery.

It took some time to dislodge the first upright and we then had an oblong aperture about two feet six inches by nine inches. Dislodging another upright gave us a further nine inches and we were able to crawl through.

Fortunately for Alec and me, there were no occupants. The area we entered was roughly four feet square and was closely timbered. The floor was also timbered and the whole place resembled a long box. A gallery so timbered would be able to withstand anything except a mine directly underneath it. We had holed near the root which meant that we had a drop of about two feet to enter. As Alec was crawling through I made a small hole so that we could shade our candlelight, and then crawled through after him. It would certainly be safer in the captured gallery and we would be able to move.

Whilst Alec, armed with a pick, kept guard at our side entrance, I crawled cautiously along towards our own line to see it any Turks were there. I kept a very firm hold of my shovel in the dark; I might have to use it if I met anyone and it was all I had to fight a war with. After crawling for quite a time, to my great relief I came to what must be the end. Satisfied that there was no one at home, I crawled back to Alec who was also sitting in the dark. I said I thought the end of the gallery was only about twenty feet from our firing line. It did not have the feel of having been recently dug and must have been there for quite a while. It appeared to run parallel with our No. 3 gallery and was probably used as a listening post. But where were the listeners – not that we wanted to meet them at the moment?

In our excitement and fear – yes, fear – it was difficult to estimate the time we had been in possession before an officer arrived. I think it was about an hour – certainly not less; it seemed a year to me. After much puffing and blowing he managed to crawl through to us. Revolver in hand, he seemed. to make as much noise as possible though he would not let us even whisper. On his way through the rabbit hole he managed to put out our nicely shaded candle. He flashed his torch continuously and had one of us in beam all the time.

This went on for some time as if he could not make up his mind whether we were friend or foe. He never uttered a word and would not let us talk. The weird silence was broken by the sound of footsteps coming along from the Turkish direction.

Nearer and nearer they came and seemed to be very loud on the wooden floor. I could see Johnnie Turk quite plainly. At least his legs and feet were clearly visible in the beam from the light he was carrying.

Every second I expected the officer to use his menacing revolver. Was he waiting, as the old soldiers tell us to, until he could see the whites of the Turk's eyes before he fired? Or, maybe, a revolver shot would make too much noise and attract attention. Perhaps the officer was going to use the dagger he had in his stocking; that would be the quietest way!

Johnnie was only a few yards away and, as I tightened my grip on my shovel, I felt the officer bracing himself for the *coup de grâce*.

'This is it' I thought and moved slightly towards the Turk, who was now almost within reach. I felt for the officer but it was Alec whom I touched – the officer had fled. Johnnie Turk, hearing the noise also fled, leaving Alec and me alone in the dark.

It took some time for us to find our side entrance. I actually found the opening but it was Alec who suggested I should go for help. I refused to go until Alec had scrambled back into the rabbit hole. He would remain to keep watch in the dark, armed with his pick, whilst I crawled along the burrow to get aid.

I had hardly begun my crawl when a terrific crack halted me. I could not understand what it was. There was another crack and then another. It suddenly dawned on me that I was being fired on from our gallery.

Not daring to move, I called out who I was and had to call many times before getting an answer.

'What the hell are you doing there?' – not very complimentary but most soothing, I can assure you.

'Hold your fire!' I shouted. 'Where the hell do you think you are? At the bloody fairground?'

'Come on out and let me see you,' said the voice.

I continued to crawl to where it was high enough for me to walk. With his rifle levelled at me all the time the soldier held me at a distance until he was satisfied I was a sapper. My goodness, it took all sorts of declarations to convince him, which in the circumstances was understandable as he told me that the officer had ordered him down the gallery and told him not to be afraid to shoot. He hadn't said anything about Alec and me; perhaps he thought we had been captured!

I asked the soldier to go to the line and bring down as quickly as possible as many bombs as he could get hold of. 'Bring a few men with you as well,' I said.

I 'borrowed' his rifle and went back to Alec who was by now in the Turkish gallery again. I had collected a couple of candles on my way in and, whilst I stood guard with the rifle, Alec arranged them so that we could see our way in and out of our own gallery.

In the meantime the bombs arrived and Alec handed them through to me. He also instructed the soldiers – without any authority of course – to fill some sandbags which he had dragged through the pipe. Goodness knows how he managed, but he had. I erected a kind of barricade across half the gallery to give myself some cover and also to protect our side door. A couple of the infantry crawled through and took over the guard post.

Now we had three rifles and plenty of beautiful bombs we were ready for Johnnie it he tried to recapture his gallery.

Alec and I began to enlarge our rabbit hole. The filled sandbags were grabbed by the chaps on guard and the barricade was soon a formidable barrier. We now had plenty of help and plenty of sandbags so we got cheeky. We advanced the barricade about five yards and when our reliefs arrived there was still no sign of Johnnie Turk.

I was not sorry to leave but was much distressed that we had not succeeded in reaching No. 3 gallery. We were so near – only a few feet beyond that wall of solid timber our pals might still be alive. We were thankful to be alive ourselves. Had we been an hour later in breaking through or had the Turk we saw and frightened away been an hour, or even much less, later on his tour of inspection, we would have had a firing squad waiting for us and no hope of survival.

Back at our advanced base in the gully we were so tired and so miserable that we did not bother to make a meal. It would have been a full-time job anyway as the rock-hard biscuits had to be soaked first. It was otherwise impossible to eat them. When reasonably soft, the doughy mess could be put into a jam tin, then prodded down the centre with a not very clean finger – which probably gave it additional flavour, to make a recess for a blob of apricot jam with genuine fly flavouring. The jam tin with its new contents would then be placed in our billy-can with as much chlorinated water as could be scrounged.

I know mother used to say that the water must be boiling before you put in the tea but she was never on Gallipoli. The tea and sugar and bits of sacking that were always with it went in first. All that remained to do was to get the mixture boiling. The sun was fairly hot but not hot enough to boil the water in the billy-can though it certainly seemed to boil that in our water bottles. A fire,was essential and fuel needed for this purpose. This should not be difficult for we miners; at home it would be easy but though we have dug very deep, we have not yet struck a coal seam. We therefore had to make do with the prickly scrub, despite its smell. I do not know its official name though I am conversant with its unofficial one. The snipers would have a bit, of target practice when we tried to collect some of the sun-dried pieces that were lying in the open and without which we could not even start a fire.

The jack-knife, by far the most useful thing issued to a soldier with the exception of his rifle, was used to make a shallow trench about a foot long and maybe six inches deep – just wide enough to allow the billy-can to rest on it. Now for the supreme effort to start the fire. The scrub is stroked very gently so that the driest spikes fall first. It must have some connection with the feline species as it hates being stroked the wrong way but the wrong way is the right way for our purpose. It's an ill wind that blows no good and the flies enjoy drinking and bathing in the blood from the countless scratches on our hands.

Mails do not arrive at the firing line very regularly. Letters are carried about for weeks, not always because of the sentiments expressed therein but because of their value in starting a fire. Small pieces of newspaper borne by the wind are always retrieved as gifts from Heaven. I have on many occasions taken foolish risks to secure these gifts, to find that the precious scrap of paper has more likely come from a latrine than from heaven, but that in no way lessened its value. Each piece would be folded neatly until required for further use.

Now to set the world alight. The paper would be carefully crumpled and the driest of the prickly scrub arranged most diligently in a bird's-nest pattern; then the not-so-dry twigs. Matches, like everything else, were very rare. That modern invention, the flint cigarette lighter with its saltpetre-impregnated wick (if your luck was in and you had sufficient wind to keep it aglow, it would just smoulder) would be placed touching the paper. You then blew gently until the paper caught alight and then blew until you blew your blooming head off. Hopes rise with the tea leaves and bits of sacking floating on top of the water. A few seconds' pause to clear the smoke from your tear-bedimmed eyes and the flame would spitefully die down, leaving a few smouldering embers. This monotonous repetition could go on for hours. A shell or two might burst overhead and instantly the order would be given 'Stop making that smoke; you are attracting attention!' As if the Turks don't know we are about!

The tea is almost boiling again but the fire is allowed to die out; blowing ceases but the shelling does not. We have little time left and shall very soon have to leave for the front line so 'Dinner is served, my lord'. The jam and fly roly-poly is eaten first and then the tea leaves, washed down with the now well-smoked chlorinated tea-stained water which looks and tastes like iodine.

Monday, September 27th

Down in the captured gallery again we found the barricade completed, a very substantial job about six feet thick, with roughly a nine-inch opening at the root through which a sentry had his rifle.

The previous shift had begun to sap towards No. 3 gallery from our end of the barricade and we continued in that direction. The sentry beckoned me to have a look over the top.

Good Heavens! Less than ten feet away there was a Turkish miner with a queer-looking lamp, digging for all he was worth and in the same direction as us. I tried my borrowing trick again but the sentry flatly refused to let me touch his rifle.

'Mahomed has been there all the morning,' He said. 'I could have picked him off long ago but we have strict orders not to fire.'

'Do you think the Army would mind if I put my tongue out at him?' I asked. At this the sentry shrieked with laughter and, somewhat startled, Johnnie Turk looked straight at us. Gradually the obvious signs of alarm left his face and be resumed digging; so did we.

If No. 3 gallery is open, we look like meeting him again. In the meantime, so long as he does not interfere with us we must not disturb him. At the moment this is all right as we can see what he is up to, but in an hour or so he will have dug himself out of sight and out of range of the sentry's rifle, whilst he plans his next move. If he is endeavouring to connect his galleries, as we are, there is no danger of our meeting before we reach No. 3. On the other hand, as we are roughly ten feet apart, a small recess made by either of us in the other's direction would bring us near enough to blast and undoubtedly someone would get hurt. The straight and narrow path is the safest course for both of us for the time being.

Tuesday, September 28th

Nothing unusual to report today; just an ordinary day of shelling, bombing and sniping. The Turks now know to within a few feet or so where the entrance to our gallery is. Bombs are crashing into our trench; quite often one comes rolling down the incline before exploding. To us they sound like thunderbolts. The working party has suffered many casualties today.

Wednesday, September 29th

On the whole, a fairly quiet day until the early evening when the Turks began to shell the gully. It was nearly 6 pm. and our reliefs were due. We tidied up the place and made ready for the erection of more timber supports that they were bringing with them. Whilst we were doing this the working party was withdrawn to the firing line and a little later we were ordered out of the gallery,

On reaching the line we were met by our reliefs who had been held up by the shelling in the gully. We were not instructed to take up arms but all the sapper crowd were on the fire-step with the rest of the men.

With one exception, June 4th, I had never been subjected to such heavy firing. The Turks either expected us to attack or were going to attack us. Every available man was on the lookout as an attack seemed imminent, we were all ready and orders were passed along that we were to move towards the gully. This meant that we were evacuating the firing line, a strange and extremely risky thing to do as the gully takes a sharp turn at this particular point. Because of this, the support line is a considerable distance behind the firing line and we have not captured enough ground to have a real second line.

The movement along the line was extremely arduous because, from their positions on higher ground, the Turks could and did, fire along our trench. To counteract this, bridges of sandbags spanned our trench, leaving less than three feet clearance underneath and in some cases we had almost to crawl. Over the top of the trench we had wire netting, not to keep out the Turk but only his bombs. The trenches were very close at this point. Most of the bombs bounced off the netting but some got spiteful and came right through it. What a scramble when they did! The bridges that we cursed every time we had to crawl under them had their uses when Johnnie got a bomb inside the cage.

We left the line just beyond the Eastern Birdcage, as it was called, and made our way down a trench that ran alongside the gully. We were on our way to the support line when the front line was blown sky-high. Lumps of earth fell for several minutes so it must have been a large mine.

I did not hear any orders given to return to the line – or what was left of it. One seldom hears orders out here; in times like this we act on our own initiative. With one accord we turned to, find that the mine had exploded just in front of the 'birdcage' most of which had been destroyed. Two galleries in this area, Nos 6 and 7, had been used as listening posts. They had been finished for some time but they were finished now all right as we couldn't find any trace of them. The whole of this part of the line was completely destroyed but the Turks did not press the attack. They were copying our tactics of a week ago, but fortunately we had vacated the front line before his mine went off and had suffered no casualties.

The Turk is very prone to copy almost everything we do.

Quite a lot of the bombs we use we make ourselves. Jam tins are carefully salvaged and filled with small stones, glass, wire, nails – in fact any old iron we can find. We are never very precise with our fuses; they are roughly an inch-and-a-half in length and the detonators are fixed to them by a gentle but firm nip with the teeth. The lid is fastened down with a piece of wire and the bomb is ready for use.

The only bombing instructions I have ever had were quite brief, namely: first make sure the fuse is alight; it should last approximately five seconds. To ensure the best result the bomb should explode just before it reaches the ground. Allowing two seconds for flight you must hold the bomb for the other three seconds. To calculate these three seconds all you have to do is to say 'A hundred and one, a hundred and two, a hundred and three'. You must then throw the bomb in the intended direction, carefully avoiding hitting your own parapet.

Having made scores of these lethal playthings in my time I was most interested in the words used in the instructions. The choice of 'should' and of 'approximately' left me in no doubt whatever as to what to do once the fuse began hissing, and I was never any good at counting, anyway. In the excitement of the moment, bombs were sometimes thrown without the first instruction having been carried out and therefore they had not been lit. Like the cat, they came back, this time alight and with tragic results. One bright spark thought of a way to score a few points from this occasional forgetfulness by making a few bombs with very short fuses – almost instantaneous ones. We would send these over unlit and then listen to Johnnie blowing himself to pieces when he did what we had 'forgotten to do'. In less than a week he had copied our ruse and caught us good and proper in our turn.

We should have been relieved long ago. Our men were with us but it was our custom to hand over in the gallery, thus ensuring that the gallery was always occupied. Today, the galleries were all empty and we felt that we must accompany our reliefs to them. Goodness only knew what Mahomed had been up to since we left.

We could not reach the gallery by the way we left it as the firing line in between was blocked. We made our way back to the support line with the intention of going up the next communication trench. This was only partially open and we had to crawl most of the way. On reaching the line we found it, too, was in an awful state and the infantry were busy clearing it up.

If it was good enough for them to work in, it was good enough for us to crawl along and we entered our gallery to find Mahomed still digging away.

If he had only known, he had had ample time to remove our barricade unmolested. He could have captured our gallery and erected his own barricade in our front line and this would have put the cat among the pigeons!

CHAPTER ELEVEN

OCTOBER

Saturday, October 2nd

In case we got on too friendly terms with Mahomed, Alec and I were allocated to a job in No. 1 gallery. We had not entered No. 1 since we had been entombed there on the 15th.

For the most part, it was a new gallery joining the old one at the point where it levelled out It was a queer feeling to be back again in the spot that had been our grave for quite a while and might yet claim us, but we had a job of work to do. We had begun a connecting sap towards No. 2 gallery in place of the one we started before the upheaval. We could hear digging in three places – immediately in front of us between Nos. 1 and 2 galleries, approaching No. 1 direct and also at the junction of our sap connecting with the main gallery. The Turk is very close at this point and occasionally the side of the trench crumbles. We and our opposite numbers have reported all this turkish digging. The lieutenant has been down on three previous occasions but each time he has been there the nearest digging has stopped at once but the distant activity could still be heard. Today it was the same and the lieutenant was very angry. He said the digging in the connecting sap was about eight feet away and the other about seven feet away. We agreed with his estimation of the sound that could be heard now, but asked him to wait until he could hear the nearer digging. We all waited but again there was no further digging.

I could understand the officer's anger but when he said he had no intention of running the risk of spoiling weeks of hard work simply because we had the wind up, I flew off the handle and Alec also.

'If you don't do something about it, Johnnie will blow first and then you will have neither sap nor sappers left.' I pointed out that at the moment everything was in our favour. The main gallery extended six feet beyond this point, a perfect recess for our mine. We would, of course, damage part of our gallery but we would still have the connecting sap which could be pushed forward to meet the Turk before he got close enough to destroy it.

We all agreed that the enemy was roughly eight feet away. We sat quiet for a while but there was still no digging nearby.

As he was about to leave, the lieutenant said in a nice fatherly way that he knew we had had a very nasty experience in this very spot. We had had a very bad spell lately and he could understand our being a little touchy.

As usual, as soon as he had gone the digging began again. It was useless to ask him to return so we sat and watched the small pieces of earth falling from the side. While we were doing this, the lieutenant came back and brought Sergeant Webster with him. This, time the sergeant did all the talking. Apparently the officer had told him we had the wind up but he was not standing for this.

'I have known these lads since the start and am prepared to believe all they say,' he said.

The four of us sat listening – not a sound! Webster went to the far end of the gallery and began digging. I joined him, leaving the lieutenant and Alec sitting in the dark. The side did crumble a little but the lieutenant was of the opinion that this was caused by the vibration of Webster's digging. Strangely enough, Alec could not hear any digging now and said so.

Webster left with the lieutenant but soon returned, having apparently convinced him that the time was ripe as we were ordered to prepare for blasting. We had all the sandbags needed for tamping, ready and waiting. We were anxious to get the job done in case the lieutenant changed his mind. He placed the two detonators in one of the 10-pound tins of Ammonal and I carefully wrapped the cable twice round the tin, then twice round a sandbag so that we would not dislodge the detonators during the tamping. The remaining four tins I placed alongside and tucked them in with a few sandbags. We lost no time in finishing the tamping; we were anxious to get it over with, but didnt want to spoil our gallery. We used more sandbags than usual but had the job done in seventeen minutes instead of the usual twenty.

In the meantime the officer in charge of the firing line had been notified that we were about to do a little blasting and the troops in the vicinity were 'standing to'.

When I reported 'Gallery clear, mine ready' the officer fixed the wires to the battery in a few seconds.

'Stand by for the blast, men,' and down went the plunger, but nothing went up.

The astonished look on the lieutenant's face made me grin and I quickly turned away so that he could not see me laughing. He would have murdered me if he had caught me.

The situation was saved for the moment by someone suggesting that the battery was at fault. Another one was soon obtained and the wires connected.

'Stand by' and down went the plunger with a vengeance, but again nothing happened.

All the blasting was done by the lieutenant and I was the recipient of most of it. According to him, I had been in such hurry that I had dislodged the detonators.

'You and Alec will report to the Captain at Pink Farm tomorrow at 8 am.' he stormed.

'Sir, I am a soldier. I do not question your authority, but as you are addressing me I can assure you that I paid particular attention to the laying of this mine. I have laid many others and I can assure you, sir, that this mine was perfect when I left it. Moreover, I will prove it.'

The lieutenant stared at me. 'This insolence will be added to the charge,' he said.

Alec and I rushed down the gallery and began clearing the top bags. The lieutenant assisted us. We soon had enough clearance for us to crawl through and, on doing so, found that the tin containing the detonators had been cut open and the Ammonal it contained scattered on the floor. The other four tins had been stolen. We were speechless!

We had very little room – only about two feet – and we looked in vain for the actual breakthrough. We crawled backwards over the tamping and I brought with me the tin that had been cut open.

Upon reaching the firing line I asked the lieutenant if I should take it with me when we reported to the captain to the morning.

'You both have enough work to do here and cannot waste your time roaming about the Peninsula. When you do go back to Pink Farm I will see to it that you have a well-earned rest,' he said.

'That's awfully nice of you, sir,' I said and this appeared to please him, judging by the smile on his face. I reckon, though, that Mahomed was even more pleased. He had given our tail a jolly good twist, not only by split-second timing, pinching our powder from under our noses, but he was now in possession of our gallery, which makes us all square as we are in one of his. It won't be so bad so long as he keeps it; when he decides to give it up the fun will start. We must finish the connecting sap before he gets past us. It sounds as though he is slightly above our level and that's how we like it.

Sunday, October 3rd

The lieutenant has been down all day. It is obvious that we have got ahead of Johnnie but we cannot let him just keep going.

It was decided that Alec and I should go and meet him, the two sappers staying in the connecting sap. The lieutenant said that if we could make a good recess we could give the Turk a shake without seriously damaging our own sap. For the first hour we could hear the Turk digging away but then there was silence for the rest of our shift. We explained this to our reliefs before we left.

Monday, October 4th

Throughout the whole day there has been no sign of Turkish digging. Is it a trap? Is he sitting waiting for us? I think he is but have kept going towards him. We reckon he is between four and five feet above us and about the same distance short of us.

It was almost midnight when we thought we could faintly hear him digging. The sound was not nearly so loud as on the previous day. The lieutenant also heard it.

Tuesday, October 5th

During the very early hours, digging was again heard. This time it seemed to be very near. The lieutenant said we were close enough to blast and had sufficient room to do this without much damage to ourselves. He went off to prepare for the mine and arrange for the

Ammonal to be brought down. In the meantime we had the sandbags filled ready for tamping.

At 5 am. the Ammonal was brought down the gallery, 80 pounds of it 'Thirty pounds to blow the Turk sky-high and fifty pounds for him to pinch if he is quick enough,' the lieutenant said with a saucy chuckle.

Twenty minutes later I reported the gallery to be clear and the mine ready.

'Stand by, men, and hold your hats on this time!' shouted the officer, grinning like a Cheshire cat as he pressed the plunger down, and, oh, what a thump! The trench trembled and immediately afterwards there was an even louder explosion. It must have been the Turkish mine. Whether we had both been ready at the same time or our explosion had set off theirs; I do not know. What I do know is that we won the race by a split second; otherwise I would not have been able to make this entry to my diary.

After a few minutes we entered our gallery to ascertain the damage. We were unable to remain down below because of the fumes. The inevitable fusillade broke out and a real shooting match was in progress when our reliefs arrived.

It seemed safer down below but again the fumes made us all return to the line, where we remained until the firing eased and then set off to our advanced base at Geoghegan's Bluff.

Upon arrival we were told to hurry up with our breakfast as we were to return to Pink Farm Headquarters for a rest. The lieutenant had kept his word, but to case he changed his mind we forgot about breakfast and went there at once. Except for shelling it was a peaceful place. We slept in a nearby ditch for most of the day. For me it was a heavenly sleep as I was so tired.

Wednesday, October 6th

Today we began a bit of digging for our own comfort. We made funk holes much the same as those we had made to our original rest camp near the beach. They are about six feet long, two feet wide and as deep as you can manage to dig – mine is nearly three feet deep. My waterproof sheet placed over the top half and held down by lumps of rock and earth, gives protection from the sun.

We have been very comfortable today. Tea was made for us and there was a good supply of Huntley and Palmer's cast-iron biscuits, apricot jam, and a piece of cheese that could not stick the jam any more than we could and repeatedly crawled away. In such pleasant surroundings, though, it was good to be alive and I feel better already. I feel human again; instead of having to burrow like a mole I can move about in the sunlight.

We have no fixed job to do. All our meals – such as they are – are cooked for us and our conversation is becoming not only rational but interesting.

Thursday, October 7th

The vacation spirit still prevails and I have been trying to make headway with my correspondence. I have not had much chance for letter-writing lately. I receive many more letters and parcels than anyone I know; everyone in my home village seems to write to me and I often receive letters from people I cannot remember even seeing. I am always very pleased to receive a letter, however short it may be, it is always a tonic. Now that I am temporarily disengaged I will do my utmost to answer these kind people.

When news of the arrival of the mail reaches us it is always my job to go down and collect it. The lads say that it will all be for me anyway. This is a fatigue I never question and the lads are all very pleased when I arrive with it.

Friday, October 8th

Today is my birthday and I have wished myself many happy returns of the day. I know that Mother has made a special cake for me and despatched it a long time ago. Like all her weekly parcels it will be meticulously packed, with an outside covering of neatly-sewn linen. Like ninety per cent of the others, by the time it reaches me it will have been cut open and most of the contents stolen. The empty case from my birthday parcel has not yet reached me, but I will write to Mother and tell her that it arrived in perfect condition on the morning of my birthday and all the lads said what a lovely cake it was.

Maybe because it is Friday it has been a lousy birthday. Just after midnight we had a terrific storm and extremely vivid flashes of lightning illuminated the very dark night. During every flash that adjacent yet remote and unconquerable Achi Baba seemed to rise up and bloat to gigantic proportions in defiance of the elements and we poor and helpless mortals. Each thunderclap seemed to come from the bowels of this remorseless monster. The raindrops were so big that they hurt and the wind-driven sand made me cover my face.

In a matter of minutes our grave-like funk holes were filled to overflowing – sunken Roman baths with all our worldly goods floating about. There was one consolation – the biscuits would be much easier to eat! I could not resist the temptation of a bath on my own doorstep. There was no danger of losing the soap as I had not been issued with any since I landed on this God-forsaken Peninsula. The sandy soil, though a coarse substitute, had to do as usual.

The remainder of the night I walked about in my birthday suit – after all, it was my birthday – colder but much cleaner than usual.

Saturday, October 9th

We shut up shop and proceeded to the support trenches and established a base in the 1st Australian lines. We began work at noon, making dug-outs for the troops. The pattern was similar to our own galleries in the front line but not so deep, only about ten feet. It was a nice, comfortable job while it lasted and we made good use of the time. There was no fear of being blasted at any moment. Like all good things, it came to an abrupt end; we were required in the firing line and the dug-outs had to be left unfinished.

Wednesday, October 13th

Back to the firing line (we seem to live here!) as this is a new mining area we found things to be fairly quiet apart from bombing day and night. The front line is like a dog's hind leg and is subjected to enfilade fire from every direction.

We began by sapping under the parapet, leaving a foot or so of soil on top as covering. The distance we covered was governed by the proximity of the opposing trenches. On an average they were about ten yards. When the required distance has been reached, the roof is brought down – during the hours of darkness of course. The disadvantage of this method is that the bombing sap is shallow because of the absence of the wall of excavated earth that would normally have been thrown up instead of being carried away during the making, but the advantage is that the sap is made without casualty and is not easy to see owing to the absence of this earthwork above the level of the ground.

Thursday, October 21st

We have completed several of these bombing saps and our men have already made considerable headway to joining them up. However, to one particular place the Turks have a trench that juts out towards our line and as long as they hold it, they command the whole area.

Using our advanced saps, the Highland Light Infantry were able to overrun the Turks before they realised what was happening and, having captured the offending trench, made their way along a communication trench and erected a barricade. They then settled down to await the ineviteble counterattack; they did not have long to wait.

Time and time again the Turks came forward and were driven back, but still they came. Several times, groups of them managed to secure a footing to their lost trench, only to be killed or thrown back again.

The barricade changed hands many times but at the close of day the lads of the 1/7th Highland Light Infantry were in possession of all the ground they had originally won.

Friday, October 22nd

During the night we supervised the continuation of one of our advanced saps and long before dawn had a communicating trench in the newly-captured trench. The line had now been reinforced and much of the enfilading fire eradicated.

The infantry were now firmly established in their new trench and the business began all over again of cutting bombing saps. They needed the few yards these advanced saps give them to lob their bombs into the Turkish front line. Of course, it's not all one-way traffic. The Turks do the same and, suffice it to say, these positions are not conducive to good health. They are however, the nearest points to the enemy and this factor is taken into consideration when mining is in the offing. Personally, I disagree with this idea for the simple reason that whilst we have less distance to mine, these bombing saps receive almost constant attention. In the event of an attack they are the most likely positions to be overrun and many hours, days or even weeks' hard work may be in the enemy's hands in a matter of minutes. But this is the policy and so we go on.

We began to go underground at once, frequently interrupted by falling bombs or slinging a few ourselves. As time went on we established a series of short underground trenches to be used as listen-posts. They will also give adequate shelter from bomb and shrapnel splinters. The boys are very pleased with them. They will be warned in time if there is any mining going on in their area and they are confident they can deal with any attack above ground but to live and sleep in a trench that might be blown up without the slightest warning is certainly no joke.

CHAPTER TWELVE

NOVEMBER

Tuesday, November 2nd

We have changed around with our opposite numbers who have lately been engaged on the dug-outs that we had to leave unfinished in the 1st Australian lines. They have almost completed one; they have gone down to a depth of ten feet and then levelled off. We are now to make cave-like cavities with narrow entrances on both sides. It is a nice rest from the firing line for a few days. When completed they will give shelter to about thirty men or, more likely, will be commandeered by the Headquarters' staff of the Regiment occupying that part of the line.

We were able to finish this particular dug-out before returning to the firing line to relieve the rest of our squad so that they can have a few days in the support lines. Like us, they need it.

Monday, November 8th

We are a little further to the right than we were a week ago but still on the same old job – going underground from the end of the bombing saps. The line has been advanced in several places by this method. There is now not so much enfilade fire but still quite enough to make you move about with caution. In certain parts it is fatal to dally during daylight. If you must move along the line, as we have to very often; it is a wise policy to keep very low when passing exposed places, and to get a move on. On the whole, the sector is at the moment quiet and we have almost finished the task allotted to us.

Monday, November 15th

We have been ordered back to Headquarters at Pink Farm and arrived at 4.30 am.

As soon as one leaves the front line one feels that time does not matter any more and there is no sense of urgency. One feels as though the heavy burden one has been carrying has mysteriously flitted away and the brain begins to function normally again. We converse with ease about bygone days and of the future. We even have visions of returning home after hostilities have ceased. In our own minds we know it is but a daydream but it is very nice whilst it lasts. Each of us has his own thoughts, but we all know that the average life of a fighting man in this glorified cemetery is less than a month. All my original section have gone long ago. I have had a hundred and twenty rounds of ammunition blown from my chest; I have been blown up several times, even buried alive for the most part of two days, twenty-five feet beneath the soil; yet here am I still alive and kicking and daring to dream of home and all that it means to us half-crazy cannon fodder.

The Russians have an old proverb which says that everyone goes mad in his own particular way. It is very comfortable to know I am not alone on my journey. Each day, each hour, each moment must take care of itself.

The present is encouraging. All we have to do is to wait for our dixie to boil so that we can have a nice cup of tea. Sergeant Webster (he is really a Petty Officer but these Army chaps cannot understand why naval ratings dressed in khaki are in the firing line) is making his way towards us. Trust the sergeant to turn up when the tea is ready.

'Just in time; come and have a real drop of Sergeant-Major's. It's almost on the boil.'

'Thanks very much, I will. But first things first.' He called his men to one side – six from the Hood Battalion, one from the 42nd and one from the 52nd Division.

'We have been chosen to do a special job over on the Right Sector. The Royal Scots are holding the line and we are going right now. There's not a moment to lose, not even for that cup of Sergeant-Major's tea. Someone has slipped up badly. The Royal Scots are to advance tomorrow afternoon and a gallery that was finished over a week ago has been found to be thirty feet short. Come on, Webster's men, let's get the job done. If those lads advance without our mines blasting the way for them, they will be slaughtered. We have all had some of that game!'

Well, our well-earned rest was nice while it lasted, the whole two hours of it.

We were on our way to the Right Sector which was entirely new to us. It would be a change of scenery, if not of work; We arrived to the unfinished gallery a few minutes before 8 am. There was a short briefing and we set to work.

The advance was timed for 3 pm. tomorrow. We had thirty-one hours to dig thirty feet, prepare the recesses for three mines, lay them, tamp them and make sure they went off at the appointed second. One man dug for all he was worth for about five minutes. The second man cleared away the hard clay, the third man filling the sandbags and the fourth taking over the digging. At each changeover each man took over the position behind him so that the man that had been digging had a short rest before taking over with the pick.

After five hours we were relieved by the other four of our team. We were exhausted but satisfied with our progress of five feet, nine inches. With a parting shot of: 'Beat that it you can, you lazy devils' we repaired to the line and, in spite of shelling and rifle fire, slept soundly until we were awakened shortly before 6 pm.

The lads holding the line gave us a very welcome cup of tea which was much appreciated.

They did not know the real purpose of our endeavours but sensed the urgency from the fact that we slept in the firing line. Our base at Pink Farm is an hour and a half's walk away and there just was not time to go back. In the normal way we would have established a base in the support line but this job is so urgent we have no time even for this.

Down below again, we found that the lads had taken out another five feet, nine inches. This was comforting; we now knew the exact nature of the ground to be excavated and the teams were well matched. We were a little ahead of time but there was still quite a long way to go – eighteen feet, six inches, and twenty-one hours of slogging. We kept to our system but reduced the spells to four hours. By the time our reliefs took over at 10 pm. we had scooped out another four feet, three inches. A special ration party had brought up tea and sugar, biscuits and cheese. It was too late to make tea but the biscuits and cheese were delicous.

The nights are cold now and we have no overcoats and no shelter. In the daytime it is uncomfortably hot and flies worry the life out of us; at night, huge spiders, centipedes, scorpions and countless other crawling creatures are everywhere. I close my eyes and make believe they are not there until one falls on my face.

Men were moving silently about like the ghosts they were. Rapid firing broke out to the French sector and, as usual, spread across the whole front. The ghosts sprang to life and we all 'stood to' for about an hour as the guns opened up and the Turkish guns followed suit.

When the firing died down, we were at peace again and wondering what it was all about; wondering if it had really happened or had it been another dream? In any case it did not matter; there is but little difference either way.

Down below at 2 am., our rivals were inches short of our yardstick. They had only managed four feet as the going was getting tougher and we are all tiring.

Ten feet, three inches to go. We were not sorry to be relieved at 6 am., having managed three feet, six inches this spell. The lads in the line gave us some of their tea. Life was good again in spite of the inevitable apricot jam; you eat so many flies with it that the label seems a waste of paper. It does not mean a thing. The jam could be strawberry and the taste would be the same. The tin would come in useful, though, probably ending up as a bomb.

We had to take over again at ten, so hoped for a little shut-eye. The trench is like an ant-heap. Everyone is on the move though there is really nowhere to go, but still they come and go. Officers enquired our progress and received the agreed answer: 'Everything under perfect control.'

'Quiet please, quiet please.' I kept hearing these monotonous words. Half awake, I appealed to a chanting Scottie to give it a break. I would not dare record his reply; it would set the page alight. I was now fully awake and apologised to Jock.

'Och, ah dinna want nae apology; ah ken fine. Am nae greeting; ah had tae carry oot ma orders.'

Evidently he had been specially detailed to prevent us from being disturbed if possible and had apparently been successful.

I felt fit and very much refreshed. I thanked Scottie for his efforts and went down the gallery again. Here I found that our opposite numbers had kept up the pace. We were well ahead and confident that we would be in time but even so we slogged away without pause.

At one o'clock all the sappers came down. We had only a foot to go and then the recesses. From now onwards we retained the filled sandbags as we would need them for tamping.

We were delighted to have beaten the clock. The recess to hold the charge was now ready and the other chap; had made the other two galleries ready. A party from Pink Farm had brought up the Ammonal and all three mines were in position. The cables were unrolled and all that remained to be done was to connect them to the battery.

The firing line was quite crowded. I cannot say the men were anxious, but the atmosphere was extremely tense. I know the feeling but it is difficult to describe. Each man is totally unaware of those around him; he is in a world of his own and aware only of himself. He is a little afraid, not of going into action, but of himself, wondering if he will be able to control himself. Would he be able to continue to go forward when those whom he had come to know so well were falling at his side and crying out for help? Would he, after a short rush and having buried his head in the prickly scrub, have the courage to rise again and face those singing bullets that crowded the air just above him? Would he be able to keep up with the few that were left? Would he have enough courage – or madness – to still go blindly forward through the rain of red-hot lead when almost all around him had fallen? Would he survive?

These are the thoughts that have occupied my mind on many similar occasions and I have no doubt as to what is going through the minds of the men now. No, they were not anxious at the moment; they were not even in this world but in a world of their own imagination. Into those crowded minutes before the attack, a whole lifetime is gone through with a small-toothed comb. Incidents that appeared inconsequential at the time and have been forgotten long ago are caught up and held for reflection; words spoken in anger or in spite are amplified as they echo from the unseen mountains. Youth's mobility has fled. There is no escape, yet there is no fear. The mind is preoccupied with the past.

The bombardment opened with a tremendous crash and the world of dreams suddenly became a world of reality bent on destroying not only dreams and all they stood for, but mankind itself.

One desires to give advice but how can one advise? In a few moments at the most everyone would know all there was to know. Everything was ready.

'Stand by. One minute to go.'

At exactly 3 pm., three mines were exploded. The Royal Scots went forward into the shower of falling earth with bullets and shells whining overhead in both directions. Dust from the explosion of the mines and shells clouded the sky and the stench was sickening.

The call for stretcher-bearers was heard above the din and there was much activity in the line.

I could not see what was going on out in front but I knew there was much activity there also – men, young and not so young, falling to the ground never to rise again. Some would be crying for help, knowing in their hearts that they would have to wait until sunset for aid and others would be panting for breath and trying to keep up with the rest to find shelter in the Turkish trench.

The attenuated line moves forward. The enemy cannot be seen but he is somewhere out there in front, fighting for his life, deeply entrenched, as our lads stumbled blindly forward into the muzzles of his rifles.

I do not need to look; I have been through it all many, many times. The returning wounded said they had captured their objective. This news was encouraging and, satisfied that our humble efforts had assisted in some small way, we moved back to the support line. Four of our team went back to bring up the rations and we others selected a suitable place to establish an advance base.

In the comparative safety of the trench we made quite a roomy dug-out, using waterproof sheets for roofing. The ration party returned and brought some timber with them as well as the rations. We all had tea together and settled down to have a good night's rest. We had finished our special task and were very satisfied with the results.

Everything had gone to plan. The Royal Scots were by now firmly established in their new trench, although there was considerable local fighting still going on, which was only to be expected in the circumstances.

At 10 pm. we were recalled to the front line. Until this afternoon this had been a Turkish trench and there was a communicating trench running back to the Turkish line. The Royal Scots had advanced along this trench, intending to barricade it and use it as a bombing sap. During the initial attack they had overrun a Turkish gallery which, unlike ours, had its entrance in this communicating trench. They had captured two Turkish miners when they came out during the course of the afternoon our lads had lost and recaptured the entrance to the gallery many times.

This type of fighting is very deadly. You rush along the trench slinging a bomb in front of you and crouching as low as possible. Another rush and another bomb, but, before you can erect a barricade you are bombed out. You don't stand much chance when a bomb falls into a trench only about two feet wide. On come the Infidels to meet the same fate. The battle area in question is only a few yards of narrow, deep trench and it is just a question of who gives way first. Men are blown to pieces and are replaced by others. Only a few at a time are actually engaged. The dead give cover for the living, while sandbags are hurriedly thrown in front of their bodies until the barricade is high enough to replace them.

The gallery entrance is about five yards in front and in between the two barricades. Our job is to get into that gallery from this side of the barricade. The two pieces of timber we have brought with us were placed over the top of the trench. One feels safer under a sheet of newspaper than when there is no covering at all.

We began to sap and had to get underneath quickly as the constant rain of bombs was bad for our health. The filled sand-bags were eagerly awaited as the barricade was strengthened. We soon had a little extra cover and the harder we worked, the safer we felt.

No one seems to have had more than a glance at the gallery, that is, no one who is now alive. What is its direction? Does it dip gradually or steeply? Does it go towards our line and, if so, how far does it go? Maybe it is only a dug-out.

We will have to guess the gradient and the direction, taking into consideration that it has about fifteen yards to go before it passes the former Turkish firing line. We are confident that the dip will be gradual and that it has been used in times of shelling as a shelter for troops.

We governed our gradient accordingly and made fair progress. We would have gone further than we did had there not been so many interruptions by bombing but by the time our reliefs arrived we had reasonable cover.

Wednesday, November 17th

We were back in the support line by 2.30 am. We were very tired and longed to sleep. Our dug-out had been so much altered that at first glance we failed to recognise it. The water-proof sheets we had used to cover the roof were now door curtains. The roof had been timbered and covered with sand-bags. The floor was about two feet lower than it had been and was reached by a couple of sandbag steps. My goodness, the remainder of our party had not been idle. It was now a home from home.

And so to the bed that never requires making as it is already made – the good earth, covered with as many empty sacks as you are lucky enough to 'win'. An overcoat, if you have one, serves as a blanket.

The night was cold and I was too tired to dream. I was awakened by a friendly kick at about 9 o'clock on a beautiful sunny morning. Now for breakfast. I had a little less than a pint of water to last me all day or maybe much longer – you could never be sure; there was no time for a shower anyway. Some tea and sugar mixed in a sandbag – I say 'in a sandbag' but most of the bag is mixed with the tea and sugar, a rasher of oily bacon, a piece of even oilier cheese garnished with millions of flies and a good supply of biscuits made our meal. We don't often see bread. The flies are not content to remain on the cheese; perhaps there is not room for them all. They swarm to my eyes, nostrils and on my lips. They revel in the sweat on my body. Anywhere moist they take possession of but I am accustomed to their presence and antics. They can have the bacon but I insist on having the cheese. Most of the pieces of sacking and flies are skimmed off the warm, milkless tea before it is swallowed and the once-proud soldier has had his breakfast.

It was our turn to go back to Pink Farm to bring timber and tools. We wound our way through miles of trenches before reaching our base in the open country. Our timing was perfect as we were offered a jam tin full of delicious bully-beef and fly soup when we got there. It was piping hot and also I 'won' a small loaf of precious bread. They don't seem to do so badly at the base.

Back at the advanced base I proudly cut my loaf into eight slices, putting two to one side for the chaps now in the gallery and handing the remainder to those present. They did not show much enthusiasm; I admit there is not a lot in one thin slice of bread but it would keep the wolf – if not the flies – from the door and I told them so. Alec then rather shamefacedly told me that they had each acquired two loaves to my one.

'You thieving scoundrels,' I cried. 'To "win" a loaf is pardonable but to take two is downright dishonest.'

However, we are all sinners so I suggested a thieves' party. Alec and I were back in the gallery by 2 pm. The two men we were relieving said they thought we had only about two feet to go. They elected to stay handy for the official opening as if it were a fete. Sergeant Webster arrived and decided that all his team should be in on this and a message was sent to the remaining four in the support line. In less than half-an-hour, all eight sappers – in fighting mood – were in the gallery. Webster insisted on taking his turn with the pick. The clay sounded 'baggy'. We kept back the filled sandbags as we might need them soon.

The officer in charge of the line came down and Webster very reluctantly handed me the pick. Within a matter of minutes I struck timber. We had arrived! With renewed energy I hewed away enough clay from the timber to reveal the now familiar pattern of a Turkish gallery. We pulled the nine-inch upright towards us but we were too anxious and had to dig away much more earth before we could break in.

The sweat was pouring from me and I was shivering with excitement or fear, perhaps both. What would happen when I did manage to break through? The entrance was in between the barricades and the Turks could have occupied the gallery during darkness and now be waiting for us to open up when they would rush out and recapture the lost trench. A bomb, knife or bayonet thrust might be awaiting my arrival.

Alec pulled again and I loosened the upright. We peered through the crack into inky darkness and listened a while.

There was not a murmur. We soon had more uprights out and were only six inches below the Turkish level. It was now comparatively easy to prise away the remaining timber and we had captured another Turkish gallery.

The sappers hauled in the sandbags and erected a low barricade in the part that lead into 'no-man's' trench and soldiers were posted. With one end closed, we decided to find out now what was going on at the other, which appeared to extend to our original front line. The gallery resembles a long wooden box with a closely timbered roof, floor and sides. It was similar to the one we captured on Sunday, September 26th.

The officer, Webster and we eight sappers set off to reconnoitre. The noise of our own footsteps was the only distraction. On reaching the end we found a large box fitted into a recess. It had obviously been constructed more or less on the spot as it was only inches less in size than the gallery and could not have been hauled here. It fitted the recess so closely that we could not see beyond it. Near the top and facing us there were several holes an inch in diameter but no wires were to be seen.

Maybe this was not a recess? There could be a gallery behind the box. We listened for any ticking noise in case there was a time fuse but there was none. The box was much too bulky to move and, if we tried, would take hours to prise out inch by inch. There was no room to get any purchase on it so, after careful thought, we decided to break it open. At first we were cautious but there was still no ticking. We soon discovered there was nothing – it was just an empty box!

Our temperatures returned to normal. The Turks must have had some object in mind to have placed it so neatly to the recess and the holes near the top seemed to have some significance but we never found the answer to Pandora's Box. The two captured miners might have been able to let us into the secret but where they were now, I had no idea.

Thursday, November 18th

We were ordered to report at once to the officer's dug-out. What had we done wrong this time? Perhaps he thought we had pinched the mine from the mystery box while he wasn't looking. We should soon know, anyway as we entered his 'office' we were surprised at the haphazard way in which it had been constructed. Compared with our palace, it was a slum.

The officer was sitting in the dim light and, with a smile on his usually poker-face, he told us to pay attention and listen very carefully. After satisfying himself that we were attending, he began reading from a sheet of paper in front of him:

> 'The eight men known as Webster's men are granted twenty-four hours' holiday with pay for exceptionally good work done on 15th and 16th November. By order of General Davies, General Officer Commanding, Eighth Army Corps.'

He continued: 'This notice will be posted up at Headquarters and will also appear in the official news-sheet, the Gallipoli Press.'

He then congratulated us. I ventured to ask exactiy what the order meant.

'It means that you men have been granted three days' holiday. Three days of eight hours equals twenty-four hours. That's what the order says and that's what it means. Starting from tomorrow at 8 am., you can do whatever and go wherever you choose; it's up to you.

Friday, November 19th

In years to come, that is, if I live, I shall be able to say with pride that I once spent a holiday abroad on the Gallipoli Peninsula, No one will believe me but what people choose to believe is of no consequence at the moment. A holiday it was and I feel chock-full of holiday spirit. There is no other spirit available out here or, if there is, I have not even smelt it. Also there are no colourful brochures to peruse, though I very much doubt if an advertisement for a holiday in the firing line would create much enthusiasm.

Yet the weather is glorious. Life is free and easy and no one bothers to dress. As there are no women around, language is varied and unrestricted, and one can and does give full expression to one's feelings at any time of the day or night without fear or favour. Meals are alfresco; insect life is abundant – extremely active and colourful. Travelling is done on foot and at your own pace. There are no roads as such and no motorcars although around the beaches can be seen plenty of mule-drawn traffic.

The Government-owned pack-mules, with their dusky drivers, may be seen in their own special wide trench.

There is free bathing everywhere, though not many sandy beaches except at Morto Bay. Here you can wade out for quite a long way and a stranded mine lying in about four feet of water serves as an ideal diving board. If you so desire, you may swim the Hellespont, the most famous of all Straits, named after Helle, daughter of Athamas and Nephele and sister to Phryxus. It will be recalled that Nephele escaped with her two children when the sacrifice of Phryxus was demanded and the three were carried away upon the back of the ram with the golden fleece. When crossing the sea between the Chersonesus and the Sigeum, Helle fell into the sea and was drowned.

Leander, a youth of Abydos, a town a few miles up the Straits, used to swim across the Hellespont every night to meet Hero, a priestess of Venus at Sestos, known to the Thracians as Chersonese. He was guided by a lamp Hero would hang out on top of a tower. One wild night the lamp was blown out and Leander lost his way, and – like Helle – was drowned. When Hero learned of his fate, she also threw herself into the water.

Lord Byron swam across these waters and in 1807 Sir John Duckworth sailed his squadron to Constantinople but did not stay as he was short of ammunition and provisions. He feared the Straits might be refortified by the French and the Turks.

If you do not have a desire to swim in these historic waters, then look straight ahead to Mount Orkanie, reputed to be the tomb of Achilles. Beyond lie the seven cities of Troy, buried long ago.

History, ancient and modern is on your doorstep and one wonders what historians will make of this attempt to force a passage through these waters where for over 350 years no hostile ship has sailed.

The Turks conquered the Peninsula to 1358 and since 1453 they have occupied the whole of the seaway from the Black Sea to the Mediterranean. It is now over one hundred years since Sir John Duckworth sailed through. During the Russo-Turkish War of 1877-78, a British squadron went as far at the Sea of Marmora and remained there, their reason for doing so being to prevent the Russians from occupying Constantinople.

We live in a strange world. Today we are blasting this piece of land to get aid to Russia. Our submarines have penetrated the minefields but on land we have lost thousands of men and are checkmated. An advance of a hundred yards is a major operation and very costly to human lives. Only those that are involved in these battles know the suffering sustained and inflicted. People back home know only what the latest communique from the Dardanelles front tells them:

> 'British forces attacked the Turkish positions south of Achi Baba today and succeeded in driving the enemy at bayonet point from their deeply entrenched positions. Fighting went on all day and several counter-attacks were made against our newly-won positions but these were beaten off with serious losses to the enemy. Hundreds of dead lie in front of our new positions which have now been consolidated.'

It makes good reading – it is meant to – but all the dead are not Turkish, far from it.

Having won the battle and beaten the Infidel, what next?

We have gone forward for the onslaught but the Turk has beaten us to a standstill. He has not run away. He has said 'This is my garden' and thrown us out. We British cannot stand for this and we have tried again and beaten him again, but in the end we are both beaten.

Contrary to the belief of people at our far-distant Headquarters, there is a limit to human endurance. There is a limit to everything, even attrition.

Even so, life is not taken too seriously out here. What would be the use when we will not get out alive? Let me give you a close-up of these heroes, these gallant gentlemen, these men at arms of whom their folks back home are justly proud.

There are roughly 40,000 men here, living a wormlike existence in this little patch of scrub. They are comparatively safe if they remain below the level of the ground but must not show their heads above if they value them. These erstwhile up-right men move around at all times in a stooping, furtive way.

Their once schoolboy complexions have been replaced by hollow jowls and sunken eyes; their bodies emaciated. Observe them stalking each other along this gigantic labyrinth, totally unconscious even of life itself, endlessly staring at something a long way off but never able to come face to face with it. The men of Gallipoli, where the quick and the dead walk side by side.

Cast your eyes on these once-human beings, crawling on all-fours like sick animals to the latrines. All are raked with that foulest of plagues, dysentery, and whilst they are in this filthy place they are a perfect target for flies, bullets and shrapnel. Many fall there and die in the slimy filth, in front of their friends who do not have the strength to help them. Death is just a matter of time for all these men who, a short while ago, were the flower of mankind – the cream of all sections and classes of the community. Life was precious to them, but not any longer. Now they wait and wonder. To them tomorrow never comes and yesterday was years ago.

Happily the stay in this sun-baked holiday camp is severely restricted. Many visitors did not actually reach the shore. Some, who saw the cliffs but not the welcoming committee, stayed only a few minutes. Those who managed the landing quarrelled with the committee and the quarrel has been kept up ever since. The average stay is less than a month. Unfortunately the death rate is high and anyone who remains standing for more than a month is cheating fate and living on borrowed time. He is constantly reminded of this fact.

How long can one keep up the challenge? The answer is simple – just as long as Fate decrees. The cat plays with the mouse only so long as it amuses him. Here am I, after over seven months, still apparently amusing the cat. In fact I have almost come to like my benign cat, but cannot say I trust him.

Now, though, I am on three days' holiday with nothing to worry about except rifle-fire, bombs, shrapnel, high-explosive shells, mines and disease. I am free of all duties and the door is wide open. I can roam where I please and have decided on a grand tour of inspection. I shall just saunter along the line from coast to coast.

The vineyard on the left of the Krithia Road seems to be an ideal starting place. This road divides the occupied zone into almost equal sections. It runs from Sedd el Bahr to Krithia and beyond. Most of the Royal Naval Divisions battles have had this road as a directional spear. It seems to have some magnetic quality which I cannot escape. Even on holiday, I am visiting here first.

The sun had risen and there was not a cloud to the sky as, without a care in the world, I made my way along the firing line, aptly named Main Street. It was difficult to traverse so I retreated a little and proceeded along Argyle Street, through York Hill into the Horse Shoe. With such a name this place should have been lucky but Fate was playing tricks. There was a first-class bombing match in progress and I decided to wait for it to end. After twenty minutes things quietened and I went on past Boundary Road trench and into the French sector without being challenged. I was met with broad grins of welcome. I told the lads the purpose of my visit, but I don't think they understood me. However, they let me continue my way along their line. It was deeper than ours, although mostly cut from rock which meant that during a bombardment by high-explosive shells, rock splinters would fly everywhere. There were plenty of good dug-outs, superior to the very few we had. Many were made of corrugated iron. The little metal we have should be referred to as corrugated tin rather than iron.

I could now understand the reluctance of the French to leave the line and go forward. They were quite comfortable where they were, except for the enfilade fire from the Kereves Ridge which dominated the whole sector. The French had a foothold astride the southern end of the Ridge and hold the west bank of the Dere down to the Straits. I do not know the actual position they were to attack on June 4th, but I can see why it was fatal for us to attack before the ridge was cleared of Turks. Even now, five months later, the ridge dominates everything and since the Turks hold almost the whole of it, they are sitting pretty.

Incidentally, so am I. At the moment I am having my hair cut. On my way along the line I came upon a man cutting and trimming another chap's beard. I was rather hot and tired and did not want to disturb him by pushing past so I sat down and waited. The bearded soldier rose, thanked the barber and went on his way. I was offered the 'chair', a plank of wood stretched across the trench. Almost before I had sat down the barber was snipping away and chatting away as he worked. I could understand little of what he said but his friends seemed to enjoy his commentary and chorused '*très bon*'. With a delightful bow, the barber then bade me rise. I gazed timidly into a polished steel reflector and saw a head fit for a crown, all done by kindness and a pair of scissors – not even a comb.

'*Merci beaucoup, mon ami.*' We shook hands and off I went on my way.

From the ridge I kept close to the coast along the Boyau de la Plage, then the Boyau de la Falaise and finally into the open to de Tott's Battery overlooking Eski Hissarlik Point.

The beach below is known as 'S' Beach. It was at this spot that the South Wales Borderers landed on the morning of April 25th. They soon overcame the little opposition they met and firmly entrenched. They remained unmolested all day and waited for the troops from 'V' and 'W' Beaches, according to their instructions. It so happened that it was impossible to land at 'V' Beach until nightfall. The Dublins and Munsters tried many times but were mown down. Only a handful reached the shore and they were pinned behind a low bank of sand only a few yards from the water's edge. They remained in this hopeless position all day, unable to move. Hundreds of their comrades left the River Clyde which had been run ashore. Those who survived the run down the gangway were shot on the barges or were drowned in the deep water. Barges were carried out of position by the current and hauled back. More men tried and more men died. More open boats made for the shore with their forty or so occupants standing shoulder to shoulder to meet the same fate as the twenty others that had preceded them. A few scrambled ashore to join their comrades behind the sandbank but the majority lay dead in the boats as they floated with the current.

When a halt to this slaughter was called, the Hampshires were still on board the *River Clyde*.

The men who had landed on 'S' Beach only two miles away did not know what was happening on 'V' Beach. They had orders to wait and wait they did while their comrades to the 29th Division were slaughtered.

So much for conducting a battle by remote control. General Napier and his Brigade-Major had been killed trying to land at 'V' Beach. Brigadier-General Hare had been severely wounded and his Brigade-Major killed at 'W' Beach. The officer commanding the Cape Helles operation, Major-General A Hunter Weston, remained on board HMS *Euryalus* at sea and apparently had not the faintest idea of what was happening on the beaches. Sir Ian Hamilton was on board HMS *Queen Elizabeth* and very comfortable, I am sure.

The lads on the cliffs and beaches, bereft of leaders, contested every inch of ground, hoping for the reinforcements that did not arrive. The dead, the dying and the living were all mixed up and the relentless sun blazed down on them.

Out at sea, out of range, out of hearing, out of sight, out of harm's way and out of touch, on board the *Euryalus* was the man in charge of operations at this end of the Peninsula. He was probably saying, 'Why the blazes don't those chaps get a move on instead of sun-bathing on the beaches?'

However, I must not digress. I had a couple of miles to go before reaching 'V' Beach. I walked along the beach of Morto Bay but could not resist the temptation of the calm, blue sea and had a swim. It was heavenly to feel the warm water around me. The thunderstorm four days ago had certainly cooled the air but the sea was warm and refreshing. This was my idea of a holiday.

Time did not matter any more, nor did Asiatic Annie. Her friendly messages of greeting appeared to be directed towards 'W' Beach. From the

Turkish point of view the direction is not bad as there are always plenty of people on the beaches. From my point of view, far too many seem to have taken up permanent residence there. Nine out of ten of them have never been anywhere near the firing line, nor are they likely to venture that way. I suppose, though, they have their work to do and their contribution must help the general effort. I am not at cross-purposes with them but the fighting soldier can never rest. He has to work even when not actually fighting.

I reluctantly left the soothing sea and made my way across the Kami Dere that runs into the bay from the direction of Skew Bridge and up the rising ground to Sedd el Bahr. Considerable rebuilding had been done since I first saw the castle in April. I made my way through the old fort and gazed upon the camber for the first time.

It was here that a demolition party of Marines landed from HMS *Irresistible* on February 26th. On April 25th, two platoons of the Dublins landed but failed to their objective. All their officers were killed and the remaining men, mostly wounded, were rescued by the Navy.

Good old Navy. Nothing is too much trouble for them and they are always at hand when needed.

Down the cliffs I went to 'V' Beach to see the River Clyde still carrying out her allotted task. The deep water between her and the beach where so many men had died when trying to land, had now been bridged. A little further along the beach, two more vessels – the *Saghalien* and the *Massena* had been beached. Between them and the *River Clyde* there was quite a respectable little harbour, much used by small craft. 'Not much chance of stowing away on any of these,' I thought to myself.

I wandered along the cliff top through an old fort, to arrive at 'W' Beach. It was here that the Lancashire Fusiliers and a company of the Anson Battalion scrambled ashore and cut their way through the barbed wire. By sheer good fortune the boats on the left had been carried out of line and landed on a small ledge of rock under the cliff at Tekke Buma. These men escaped the terrible cross-fire brought to bear on those who had landed at the appointed spot and, from their position on the flank, were able to eliminate some of it. The Worcester and Essex regiments followed and 'W' Beach was ours. It was now a hive of industry.

I estimated that I had covered half my tour. Feeling hungry I decided to call at the hospital, where I related the happenings during my previous visit. The orderly to whom I spoke was amused but I doubt if he believed my story. However, it earned me a free lunch of hard biscuits and tea, for which latter I did not even have to sign the poison book before drinking. I thanked the orderly for his hospitality and set off again.

This time I followed the Aegean coast by way of a track skirting Hill 114 and then down the cliffs again to Bakery Beach. I had not been here before or even known of its existence but it was not much of a place.

A stiff climb up the cliffs brought me back to the tracks I had left and, still hugging the cliffs, I continued until I reached 'X' Beach.

The landing here was made by the Royal Fusiliers, Inniskillings, Border Regiment and two companies (less one platoon who were at 'V' Beach) of the Anson Battalion. The covering fire from the Navy was so effective that the infantry scaled the cliffs without loss. Having secured the left flank and front, the right flank moved southwards to establish contact with the main force that had landed on 'W' Beach but instead met the Turks who were still in their original positions around Hill 114 as the advance from 'W' Beach had been delayed because of the failure to land on 'V' Beach. They did eventually join up, though.

Incidentally, the landing at 'X' Beach had been intended to be a subsidiary attack, the main landing being at 'W' and 'V' Beaches, but we know what happened to the main force.

Leaving 'X' Beach I continued towards the line by way of Ayr Road (Cross-cut 'A') and then up Longitudinal Trench No. 1, to arrive back at our headquarters. Here I met some of my mining pals who had just returned from the line for a rest. I hope they have a longer 'rest' than we did. Ours lasted little more than an hour before we were back again in the line for that special job which earned me this holiday.

I explained how I was spending my three days and that I intended to cover the whole area of occupation. I didn't suppose anyone else had done this. I had already covered half and intended to complete my tour some time today.

They thought I was daft and told me so, but gave me a wonderful meal of real bread, Fray Bentos and a Maconochie ration, swilled down with a pint of tea. I do not wish to appear ungrateful but it does not seem right to me that the further one is from the firing line – and the safer one is – the more plentiful and assorted the food becomes.

Leaving Pink Farm I made for Gully Beach. I had been here many times before. Everything was much the same – plenty of people on the beach. I felt an intruder and hastily made my way up the Ravine to reach our advanced base at Geogheghan's Bluff. All the miners operating on the left flank are based here. I had last been here on October 5th, so felt quite at home.

I next went up the cliff and into the trench taking me to Gurkha Ravine; then on to 'Y' Ravine and 'Y' Beach. The King's Own Scottish Borderers, the Plymouth Marines and a company of South Wales Borderers landed at this spot just after dawn on April 25th and met no opposition. It was so peaceful that the troops made no attempt to entrench themselves. The Marines held the flanks, the KOSB's and the South Wales Borderers held the centre and the left flank took up a defensive position roughly facing north-east. The remainder of the force advanced eastwards, crossed the ravine and then took up a position some distance beyond but parallel with it. They remained in these positions for hours, waiting for the advance from the south which did not come. Later it was decided that as the advance from the south had not materialised, they should take up a defensive position covering the beachhead, with the right flank remaining astride the Gully Ravine to assist the advance if and when it occurred.

At dusk the Turks threatened the position and the right flank was withdrawn from across the Gully to the shore. Thus the bridgehead was an arc – both flanks resting on the sea and the centre pushed forward a few hundred yards. This would have been a good defensive position if the enemy was directly in front but they were all round the arc. No sooner had the retirement been completed than the Turks attacked in force on the left and in the centre. Bullets that missed their targets on the right flank probably found good ones on the left and vice versa.

Under cover of darkness and the dense scrub, the Turks attacked again and again. Small groups succeeded in penetrating our line, to be thrown out at the point of the bayonet. One group managed to crawl through the scrub on the cliff-face and played havoc behind our line; men were found later with bullet and bayonet wounds. The attack from the front was intensified.

Just before dawn on the 26th, the Turks broke through our line between the Marines on the left flank and the KOAB's in the centre but a counter-attack restored the position. This seemed to break the Turks' hearts as they withdrew and did not attack again.

Strangely enough, as the Turks retired, so did we. In fact, half of the force had left unbeknown to the others. Colonel Matthews and the remainder of his two companies of Marines on the left flank were unaware of the re-embarkation until it was almost complete. After collecting the wounded, he and his men re-embarked just after 9 am. on the 26th.

'Y' Beach, captured without opposition and most gallantly held for more than a day against continual attacks, was given up to an enemy who had already accepted defeat and had actually retired.

It is said that in war one must not make the same mistake twice: We made the same mistake twice in one day, again through trying to direct operations by remote control. Boats were sent to evacuate the troops, nobody knowing on whose authority, and the troops were taken away.

To sum up our failure to capture Constantinople within a week, let me glance to that fateful Sunday morning seven months ago.

The 'Y' and 'S' Beach forces outnumbered the whole Turkish force opposing the five landings at the southern end of the peninsula on April 25th. The 'S' Beach force remained inactive all day. Only two miles away, the force endeavouring to land at 'V' Beach was annihilated.

One mile further round the coast, at 'W' Beach, a landing was made at terrible cost, the troops clinging to the cliff top by their teeth. An hour's march away, roughly four miles up the coast at 'Y' Beach, two thousand men landed without opposition and sat around for eleven hours, unmolested and waiting. At dusk they were attacked and suffered heavy casualties and their line was broken. They counter-attacked and restored their position; in doing so they gave the Turks such a beating that they cleared out – but so did we. Most of the officers had been killed or wounded and the luck was with the Infidel.

How dreadful that so much gallantry and sacrifice was wasted because of the absence of information on what was happening on the other beaches. Troops were poured into the death trap on 'V' Beach when everyone on the spot knew it was hopeless. The troops were withdrawn from 'Y' Beach instead of being reinforced even though there were other troops still in the transports cruising off shore.

No, you cannot win a battle of this nature by remote control from a ship at sea. The Turks did not beat us! We beat ourselves! Our commanders were out of touch, out of date and out of sympathy.

I had finished my tour of the beaches and what I have related above is what men who took part in the various engagements told me on the spot and within days of the landings. I feel that the whole story must be told so that there can be a general picture of the nature of the operation, the terrain, the difficulties and – above all – the lack of leadership at vital moments. The price paid was a heavy one. I had to be on my way as I still had a long way to go. Retracing my steps at 'V' Ravine, I proceeded by way of Gurkha Mule Trench beyond Bruce's and Essex Ravines into the Western Mule Track which took me past the Border and Trolley Ravines into the Salford, Rochdale and Bury Echelons to finally reach the firing line.

I made my way along Fifth Avenue to Fusilier Bluff at the extreme left of the line. It looked like the end of the world, with dense scrub everywhere and ravines ahead and behind.

Looking out to sea, I could see nothing but the island of Imbros; all the ships had gone home. I turned my back on the sea and retraced my steps along Fifth Avenue, where the trenches are very close.

Western Birdcage is, as its name implies, a stretch of trench with a birdcage of wire overhead to prevent bombs crashing in. It has proved a very effective system.

On I went along Forward Inch to Halfmoon Street which wraps itself around the Gully Ravine, bends back towards the sea and, then goes up the other side to the Eastern Birdcage. The Eastern Birdcage is similar to the Western but here the Turkish trenches seem even closer.

I then went underneath the Northern and Southern Barricades, along the New Cut into the Rue de Paris and underneath the Worcester Barricade. These barricades are sandbag bridges over the firing line, their purpose being to prevent enfilade fire along the line. Without these barricades the line could not be held because of the enemy's position. We have bitten into his lines in the centre but the flanks are still behind. These flanks are on higher ground and the Turks could fire from them along our line but for these barricades.

I continued along the line at Forest Road. I could not see any trees but the Turkish line here is extremely near ours. I reached the Krithia Nullah. I went another short distance before crossing the right fork of the Nullah into Cathedral Street which brought me to the vineyard held jointly by the Turks and ourselves. This was where I had begun my grand tour.

I arrived back home in the support line east of Achi Baba Nullah just before midnight. I was very satisfied with my first day's holiday as I had achieved all I had set out to do.

Saturday, November 20th

I felt very stiff so joined the ration party to work it off. Soon the stiffness was forgotten but the ragging began. It was all good natured of course. When I spoke of the various places I had visited, the chaps were really interested and asked many questions. Had they finished so and so gallery? Was the old dug-out on the side of the gully still in use?

I was able to answer most of their enquiries and felt my tour had been worth while. In one way or another I had fought in every section of the front except the extreme right. The French took over this section when they were withdrawn from Kum Kale on the Asiatic side on April 26th. On many occasions we have assisted the French in recapturing lost trenches; we were even loaned to them for a while and fought under their command.

Most of my pals are buried in the places I visited yesterday; I wanted to say 'Goodbye' to them while I could. Throughout my tour I fought the battles over again. Time and again I saw and conversed with the dead. I saw their wives, mothers and sweethearts. All the time I wondered why I was stifl alive and thanked God I had been spared to make this pilgrimage. God willing, I shall do it again.

Sunday, November 21st

The final day of my holiday. I have made headway with my correspondence; the folks back home will be pleased I have had this break.

I then went off to Morto Bay for a swim. I might have to go without a wash for weeks so I made the best of this opportunity. The sea was still warm. The weather is quite hot in the day but is cold after sundown; very similar to the weather we had to April.

Whilst I was sunbathing on the beach, Asiatic Anne began strafing so I made my way back to the support line. There is no peace anywhere in this cemetery.

After writing one more letter, I took a casual stroll to where the Royal Naval Division are holding the line. I found the Hood Battalion but did not come across anyone I knew. A little disappointed, I returned to my own sphere of operations.

I was curious to know what was being done about the captured mine gallery. I soon found out – absolutely nothing!

The barricades had been strengthened both to the communication trench and in the gallery, but the gallery itself was as I had left it. I had hopes of a well-organised dug-out with an entrance to our original front line. It seems extremely dangerous to me to leave it as it is. If either barricades are overrun it will be a simple matter for the Turks to come down the gallery and plant a mine almost directly beneath our support line, but no one seems interested in this fact – or perhaps no one cares? Maybe no one is capable of caring any more what happens!

At the moment the Turks are shelling our front lines. They have not eased up during the last hour and a half. Their aim is uncomfortably accurate – not surprising as this trench was theirs a few days ago.

Rifle fire broke out and I left the gallery to take up a position on the fire-step. The Turks are attacking on a wide front, covering the whole of the sector held by the 52nd and the Royal Naval Divisions. Line after line of the Turks have come and been mown down but they are still coming forward. None have reached our lines, though some got fairly close.

Soon it will be dusk. The sun is low in the sky and in the fast-approaching darkness the usual pattern will emerge. Those of the wounded who have survived the torture of the blazing sun and are able to crawl will try to reach their own lines. Many will have lost all sense of direction, time and purpose and will crawl about aimlessly in No-man's-land. Our chaps, not being able to distinguish between a wounded man driven almost mad by pain and thirst and a man crawling to attack, will fire at anything that moves in the scrub in the darkness. The Turks, fearing we are going to attack, will reply and most of the poor devils that have lain out there for hours waiting for darkness and a chance to five, will to the end die only a few yards from the comparative safety of their own trench and probably from bullets fired by their own countrymen, maybe even their own pals.

This is not fantasy – it is real. I have seen it so often. A figure approaching you during darkness from the direction of the enemy is an enemy and must be treated as such if you want to live yourself. It goes on all the time – self preservation. After an attack has been beaten off. No-man's-land springs into life during the night. The scrub and stones move and the dead come to life. There is movement everywhere and tension is high. It is not a dream, yet things are not what they seem. Imagination runs wild and makes fools of us all. The day's events distort the mind and the brain becomes dull. It is befuddled, stunned, and ceases to reason. The shocks of the-day are followed by a form of mental paralysis. The night is a long, drawn-out nightmare and sleep comes only through sheer exhaustion.

Monday November 22nd

My holiday over, I have begun work again. I enjoyed the holiday and have benefited from the rest and change. The shelling of the front line yesterday did considerable damage but the infantry have done much to the way of repairs and we are now able to continue with our task of making saps towards the Turkish front line. Compared with yesterday, today is quiet – but very busy.

Thursday, November 25th

We have been on the move again, through Wigan Road, Ardwick Green, Right Avenue, Twelve Tree Copse, Lancashire Street and down the Zig-Zag into the Gully Ravine and up the other side to arrive again at Geogheghan's Bluff. We dumped our belongings and proceeded at once to the firing line between the Eastern Birdcage and the Northern Barricade. There are several mine galleries in this area and we have been instructed to make recesses in readiness for blasting should the occasion arise. Past experience tells me the occasion will soon arise. However, we shall await developments.

Friday, November 26th

I have been working today in what is known as Beri's Sap on the left of the Gully. It is a special job and we have been brought into this sector to put the finishing touches to it. Considerable work has already been done; a gallery has been driven down very close to the edge of the Gully and we now have to go forward parallel with the cliffs and keeping as near as possible to them. Measurements have to be taken almost continuously to prevent our breaking through prematurely. We have a long way to go – beyond the Turkish firing and first support lines, getting beneath that part of the support line which is in the Gully. The Turkish firing line in the Gully is only a short trench but the redoubt and the mass of barbed wire have made the position unassailable.

Our own lines are well advanced on both sides of the ravine but the Turks are firmly established to the wire in the bed of the Gully. A frontal attack is out of the question as the cliffs are almost perpendicular. Some other way has to be found and this is our job.

As we are additional staff to the Geogheghan Base, we had to make a dug-out and whilst we were in the gallery our reliefs made a start by cutting into the cliff side, an excellent position for a shell-proof shelter. It will take time and a lot of hard work but as we are likely to remain in this sector for a considerable time, we would like a decent dug-out. There is plenty of timber for use in the galleries lying about which we can 'borrow'. You are never given anything here; you just bide your time and, when no one is looking, borrow what you need and keep your mouth shut when enquiries are made, often joining in the search for things you yourself have 'borrowed' weeks ago.

Our opposite numbers had made a good showing and we set about fixing up some sort of temporary shelter for the night. The wind from the south was very cold and increasing all the time; we have not had such a cold wind before.

By dusk it began to rain. We were without shelter and the tempo of the storm was increasing. By midnight a full gale was blowing, with torrential rain. The trench we had dug to the cliff side, like those on the slope, was now non-existent, filled in or washed away by the raging torrent. Stores, timber, equipment, bodies – some fresh, some decomposed – pieces of uniform with bones protruding, floated past as the rain and shelling went on without a pause. Men were standing around, soaked through, as all available shelter had been swept away. Waterproof sheets flew through the air like overgrown bats and we had the utmost difficulty to keep our feet to the raining sea of mud.

Saturday, November 27th

With the dawn we were amazed at the devastation around us; it was unbelievable. In the vast quagmire, hundreds of men stood stupefied and shivering in the uncanny silence, A few hours ago it would have been fatal to expose oneself above the earthworks for a fraction of a second, yet here we were, oblivious of danger, just standing in the open, bewildered. The elements had beaten us.

The wind and rain showed no sign of abating so we struggled up the slippery slope in an attempt to reach part of the firing line situated on higher ground but every trench was blocked with debris. We tried to go forward along the gully and covered a hundred yards after an hour's struggle. Here there was so much debris that it had blocked the usually dry bed and beyond the dam a huge lake extended as far as the eye' could see. Time and time again the dam would give way, releasing its flotsam – boulders and bodies – in a mad rush to the sea, but another dam would form some distance further down the twisting ravine.

We were almost back where we began and realised it was a waste of time and effort to try to get to the firing line to relieve our men. We struggled through the mud in the direction of our base and had difficulty to finding it. The whole face of the cliffs had changed and to many places water was cascading over the top, forming small gullies, Geogheghan's Bluff resembled a sewer outlet to the sea.

Having reached higher ground, we set about trying to make some shelter from the wind and rain. We cut into the hillside, using the earth to form a Barrier, but the rain washed most of it down the hill. After hours of hard work we managed to make the screen high enough to give a little shelter.

At dusk the rain, which had been continuous for twenty-four hours, ceased and the wind veered round to blow across the Gully. It was very cold. Half an hour later a few snowflakes fluttered down and the wind, coming now from the north-east, gradually increased. The rain changed to sleet and by midnight a fierce blizzard was raging.

Sunday, November 28th

After midnight it seemed to be even colder. The wind eased a little and the snow – now quite heavy – began to settle. The ground was frozen hard and the flooded trenches and pot-holes were covered with ice. Men froze to the ground; No one had any winter clothing; in fact no one had any underclothing at all, except maybe a spare shirt.

When we moved to this sector I wore my spareshirt, it being the easiest way of carrying it. We had to go at once to the firing line and I had no time to take it off but after one spell in the gallery I was able to undress for a while. How pleased we had all been when the rain began. I collected enough in a biscuit tin to have a bath, using one of my shirts as a towel.

There was no hope of getting dry as the rain was so heavy but I found the rub-down refreshing. I enjoyed standing naked in the rain, not knowing then of course that it would not cease for twenty-four hours and then turn to snow. The bath would have been more efficient had I some soap but I have seen none since arriving here seven months ago. Had I received any, I probably would have eaten it! After bathing I put my spare shirt in the water to soak and now it is frozen solid.

I was stiff with cold but hoped my walk to the front line would thaw me. The conditions in the line were heartrending. The poor devils were in a sad state and it was pitiful to watch them trying to work the frozen bolts of their rifles with their numbed hands. Our only consolation was that the Turks must be in a similar predicament. Any thought of attack was out of the question at the moment; both sides were licking their wounds.

The frost and the icy wind showed no sign of abating and I was thankful to have work to do down the gallery which we refer to as 'Dean's Tunnel'. The infantry were also thankful to escape the rain and wind. There could not be many men in the line as they all seemed to be in the gallery but there was sufficient work for them all. Four crews of sappers, eight men in all, were digging for all their worth. One pair were pushing straight ahead, another pair making their way underneath the Turkish support trench and the others were heading for the gully.

Our reliefs arrived, having been to the beach for the rations. They considered they had been lucky to get anything. The raging seas had washed the piers away and the beach was strewn with the wreckage of smashed boats. Shreds of tarpaulins and tents adorned the cliff face.

Back at the Bluff we set about remaking our dug-out and by nightfall had made considerable progress. We had some shelter from the howling wind, at any rate for the time being.

Monday, November 29th

We went in the early morning for the rations, if any. The sea was playing havoc with the remains of the pier and hundreds of men were carrying rocks to it in an attempt to save it from becoming a total loss. The sea was taking away the newly-placed rocks as though they were marbles and drenching the men!

We made several journeys for driftwood for our shelter. We could not let this opportunity slip away as there was enough wood lying around for us to make ourselves the best dug-out on the peninsula. We would need it, too, as the frost showed no sign of becoming less severe; in fact it seemed to be colder than ever.

Tuesday, November 30th

The walk to the front line has become even more arduous. We have not much strength left and need to rest more often on the way up. Before the deluge we could manage the walk in one stage but not now. Everyone is the same; exhausted men are to be seen all over the place. I fear some will not last out the day.

We eventually arrived in the line and relieved our chaps in the forward position after a long walk underground. I felt comfortably warm for the first time in several days. The snow had ceased but it was still very cold.

Nothing unusual happened in the gallery during our turn of duty. We did quite a lot of measuring which somewhat retarded our progress but on the whole we had made good headway when our reliefs arrived just before 6 am.

An officer told me that at the moment there were fourteen degrees of frost. This will knock all that dysentery for six,' he said and wandered along the line to give his frozen ghosts the glad news.

CHAPTER THIRTEEN

December

Wednesday, December 1st

Another very cold night but the rising sun brought warmer weather. A general thaw then set in, causing flooding everywhere. Conditions were soon dreadful – every trench had its own stream. The constant passage of heavily laden men soon turned the streams into treacherous quagmires from which there was no escape. Only the strongest managed to plough their way through. Many remained stuck in the mud, too exhausted even to try to extricate themselves; they were a sorry sight.

Many will die and slide beneath the slime to be trampled upon by those that follow who are unaware of their existence. The list of the missing will be a long one. It is much too long already but there is nothing anyone can do except weep. Even then, one cannot obliterate the scene. Tears will not wash away the ghastly, indelible panorama.

After another spell of four hours in Dean's Tunnel and two more wallowing in the quagmire, I reached the forward base on the hill in beautiful sunshine.

My spare shirt – actually my whole wardrobe – was still firmly embedded in the ice but the tin had bulged at the sides and I was able to coax the ice-block to slide out. I made a small gantry and placed the ice where the sun would melt it, putting the biscuit tin beneath to catch the drips. I soon collected enough water to make tea for the six of us. We thoroughly enjoyed it, proclaiming it to be the best tea we had tasted for a long time.

We then got on with the job of diverting the muddy stream of water away from our near-perfect shelter by way of a comparatively shallow trench dug right round our abode. Should the rain come again we were confident that our extra work would not have been in vain.

It was pleasantly warm now. My ice-block had melted and my shirt was free. I spread it out so that it would get the full sun and soon dry. I sat by, basking in the sun and enjoying life. When I casually turned my shirt I had a shock – lice were crawling all over it! After three days encased in ice they should have been dead but they were extremely lively, thanks I suppose to the high quality of my blood on which they had thrived, much to my discomfiture.

During my sojourn here I have had many varieties of tea, the most common of course being fly tea. Other brews have tasted of petrol, oil, bully-beef, sandbag hessian and chloride but I never thought that my best mug of tea would be flavoured by lice. Anyway, we didn't eat them!

Thursday, December 9th

We are still working in Dean's Tunnel on the left of the Gully. There has been no sign of counter-mining by the Turks. We have made good progress; the forward position is just beyond the Turkish support line and the second gallery is now deep enough to go forward underneath it.

The most important event of the day was the receipt of our first issue of butter. It has taken seven and a half months for someone to realise that something greasy to spread on the cast-iron biscuits does help them on their way down our parched throats. Each man received a pat the size of a half-crown, maybe not quite so thick.

We all enjoyed our rich living. Now we shall win the war, in spite of the rain! I hope we get some more butter tomorrow but I doubt it This mollycoddling might upset morale or soften us. We might even ask for eggs next!

Friday, December 10th

We have reached the limit of our forward position and my pal and I have been given a job in one of the side galleries being driven towards the Gully. According to the last measurements we had some distance still to go.

After about two hours' work the earth sounded 'baggy' and we reported this at once as we knew it meant we were about to hole. In fact, while we were waiting for the officer-in-charge to arrive the earth gave way and we could see daylight – just a faint glimmer. We at once erected a barricade in case of further falls of earth.

If the Turks had observed this opening in the cliff side in between their lines our months of hard work would have immediately become useless. There was also the potential danger to our own lines. Someone had to take the blame. We should have stopped digging sooner even though our measurements told us we had several feet to spare. We should have sent for authority much earlier notwithstanding the fact that our gallery was the least advanced of three similar ones. It was because of this backwardness in comparison with the other two that we had been given the job of bringing it into line ready for the great day.

Sunday, December 19th

All was now ready for the attack. During the last few days we have placed nine explosive charges in position, three underneath the Turks' support line, three in the cliff side beyond and three in the cliffs to front of this support Line. At the thrust of the plunger the Line would go up and the side of the Gully come crashing down. We had three short galleries leading from the main one that could be broken through into the Gully in a matter of minutes.

As I have said, an attack from the front was out of the question by virtue of the terrain and the impassable mass of barbed wire. The attack had to come from behind the Turkish front line.

The galleries were full of the troops who were to lead the attack – the Highland Light Infantry of the 52nd Division. We broke through into the Gully simultaneously with the exploding of the nine mines and the troops rushed through whilst the earth, was still showering. They were unable to get far across the thick barbed wire and machine-gun fire from the centre of it held up any further progress. Yard by yard the troops crept forward and managed to obtain a foothold in the short trench leading to the redoubt where the machine guns were positioned whilst others dug a shallow trench half-way across the Gully.

While this was going on we erected a sandbag screen in front of the openings used by the troops to prevent the Turkish machine-guns on the opposite heights from dominating the only means we had for the moment of getting our troops into the Gully.

The forward trench changed hands many times. Bombing raids dislodged our men and by the same tactics they dislodged the Turks. The bed of the Gully with towering cliffs on either side confined the operation yet some of the fiercest fighting of the campaign took place. Losses on both sides were severe. The battleground was not as large as a football pitch, was covered with barbed wire, and there was no retreat for either side.

By nightfall the lads had captured most of the trench leading to the centre of the machine-gun nest and erected a barricade a few yards from it.

Monday, December 20th

We began mining from just behind the barricade in the newly-captured trench. Normally we go underneath the parapet but as the redoubt extends down the Gully, much of it is to the rear of us so we had to go underneath the parados. Almost at once the Turks sent over a shower of bombs from all directions – over the barricade, over the parapet and over the parados. Our men retaliated. My pal and I were in the way so we moved a little further along the trench to collect some timber we had left there. During a lull in the bombing we used some of this timber to form a shelter over the spot where we were to commence mining.

By the time we were relieved we had managed to make a fairly respectable entrance to our gallery. The bombing chaps claimed the filled sandbags to strengthen their barricade. This suited us as the stronger they made it, the better. It was most unhealthy in the trench with bombs falling like rain. I would have preferred to be on the fire-step where I could see what was coming and act accordingly. Throughout the afternoon the chap who was not actually digging had to be ready with a partly filled sandbag to smother bombs falling into the trench – not an easy task when several bombs came at once, as they often did.

Tuesday, December 21st

We were back to the gallery at 2 am. and instructed to turn left with our digging. We had gone down very steeply and were now deep enough to make for the redoubt. We estimated it would take us about a week to get underneath the centre of it.

All morning the Turks shelled the Gully. They seem to have plenty of shells now; quite a lot of heavy stuff has come over. As a consequence, our reliefs were delayed and we were late in going back down the Gully.

It is now 6.30 in the morning and rain is falling heavily.

We have to be back in the gallery at 2 pm.; four hours' work down below and eight hours out of it, but by no means resting. Travelling to and from the Line takes quite a time and there are many things to do such as collecting the rations, scrounging for firewood, and carrying timber and sandbags for use in the galleries. We do not get much time to ourselves.

Our shelter at Geogheghan's Bluff is quite dry despite the heavy rain; apparently our drainage system works.

We dined on the usual bully-beef stew and then made our way up the Gully and relieved on time. We now have quite a respectable gallery. The only fault is that an occasional bomb rolls into it, but as we have turned left they have plenty of time to explode before reaching us. We originally placed a couple of sandbags at intervals down the slope but people fell over them in the dark. We then made a recess where the gallery turned left.

It is quite a change to be able to get on with the digging without being molested. The bombing goes on all the time of course but by now it is so familiar that we ignore it. It is said that one can get used to anything, except hanging.

The time passed very quickly and, our shift over, we made our way along the forty-yard front Line where the troops were 'standing to' in an uncanny silence. On surfacing in the firing line on top of the Gully by way of Dean's Tunnel we were faced by a couple of Dublins' bayonets. Having satisfied themselves we were not the enemy, they whispered to us that the Turks were about to attack. This pre-knowledge amused me; the Turks do not usually send a postcard to let us know of their intentions – it is usually just the opposite. One of the Dublins beckoned me to have a look and, sure enough, the Turks were crawling about in front of their own firing line. They appeared to be coming out of their Line from underneath the parapet, copying our tactics again. There was no one to be seen yet coming over the top but the scrub to front of their line was full of crawling men and we were waiting for them.

The rain had ceased but the sky was overcast. Darkness was almost upon us and, by the look of things in front, so were the Turks. There were boxes of bombs everywhere and each man had one in his hand ready to strike. Everyone was remarkably cool and composed; just anxiously awaiting the attack. The bombs were of an improved jam-tin type. A band of material was wrapped around one's forearm, on which was sewn a small strip on which to strike the fuse in the same way as one would strike a safety match. The thrower had five seconds to get rid of the bomb provided the fuse had been cut to the correct length. One is always thankful if the fuse is at least long enough for you to throw the bomb. They are not always but the main purpose of a bomb is that it should go off and kill or wound someone. Whether the victim is the enemy or the thrower does not seem to be of any concern to the maker.

Shortly after 6 pm., the crawlers were on their feet and coming towards us – hundreds of them. In a matter of seconds they were within fifteen yards of our firing line and into a rain of jam-tin bombs, not one in ten of which exploded – they had apparently got wet. The striking material was also wet and useless.

Without waiting for orders, the Dublins were over the parapet in a flash and met the oncoming Turks with their bayonets. I have often read that when the British Tommy shows his bayonet, the enemy turns and runs for his life. Not so the Turk; he is as plucky as you will find anywhere in the world. Instead of taking flight he took possession of our trench in several places only to be slain or taken prisoner.

The battle went on in No-man's-land for over an hour. In my sector, near the Gully, it ended somewhat curiously. I suddenly realised that the fighting had ceased except for a personal bayonet fight between a Dublin and a Turk strictly according to the rulebook, each parrying the other's thrust. First the Dublin had a slight advantage, then clever footwork gave the advantage to the Turk. Both bayonets were pointing to the Sky, then pointing to the ground. Advantage to the Irishman; the Turk, pushed him away; both thrust both parried and so it continued until both men sank to their knees, absolutely exhausted. They faced each other, gasping for breath, with determination on their faces but no sign of anger. After a few moments we moved forward to collect our men and the Turks did likewise. We were within arm's length of each other but no one spoke. We, and they, hauled our men to their feet, both still holding their rifles at the ready. Both parties turned and walked slowly away to their respective trenches. Not a shot was fired from either line even though there were at least a dozen men ambling about at point-blank range. As we assisted our lads over the parapet, the boys gave a resounding cheer for the safe return of their conquering hero. I am certain I heard a similar cheer from the Turkish line.

Friday, December 24th

Yesterday the Turks bombarded the extreme left flank all day, not only the forward trenches but the 'rest camps' and the beaches. Today they are shelling the right centre and appear to be keeping to the same pattern – systematic shelling of one sector at a time, front line to the beaches, all day long.

Saturday, December 25th (Christmas Day)

A day of rejoicing for all the civilised people of the world. A day of feasting, goodwill, compliments and presents. A day of family gatherings reminiscing on the bygone years, recalling the good and happy times but inwardly anxious felt peace and the return of those who are dear to them. In their hearts is the constant fear that their dreams of normal family life will be shattered with the morning's post.

We do not have to wait for the post. For us there is no rejoicing and certainly no feasting. The only presents we are receiving at this moment we can well do without – they are far too destructive.

The Turks are concentrating on our sector today. Someone has given them lots of guns and ammunition but by the sound of them they are much too big to have been brought down the chimney. I have a feeling that all this shelling is a prelude to an attack. The question is – where will it be made? I do not think we shall have to wait long to find out. These last three days the British sector has borne the brunt but the French have been left severely alone.

Winter conditions have set to with almost continuous rain. It is very cold after sundown. As the officer forecast, the flies have gone and taken the dysentery with them but, even so, very few men are fit; all are weary and tired. As long as you are able to stand upon your feet you are considered fit to remain and fight. It takes much longer to do anything or get anywhere nowadays even in the infrequent lulls between shelling.

Late in the afternoon, whilst down in the gallery, we were alarmed by exceptionally heavy detonations overhead. Since the working party had not been down for some time to drag away the results of our efforts, my pal and I decided to investigate.

The Turks were heavily bombarding our line. We could not see any of our troops as we cautiously peered from our gallery entrance. We thought that surely there must be someone around but there was not a single man to be seen in the forty-yard long firing line.

The Turks were blasting the side of the Gully with high-explosive shells with the apparent object of preventing anyone entering or leaving the line by way of Dean's Tunnel, the only way in or out. We were stranded! Two almost naked sappers cornered like a couple of rats only a matter of a few yards from the Turkish redoubt that bristled with machine-guns. We took what shelter we could find behind the deserted barricade and armed ourselves with a couple of bombs each from boxes to a recess nearby.

The shelling was the heaviest I had known but we were so close to the Turkish redoubt that we were, so to speak, out of range. If the Turks shelled us they must also hit their own men in the redoubt. We decided that because of their own shelling the occupants were lying low and hoped they would continue to do so. We kept quiet on the assumption that if we started a bombing match they would retaliate. As long as the Turks continued shelling our front Line there was no danger of an attack.

After what seemed a lifetime the shelling abruptly ceased. Now for the attack! Against the whole Turkish army stood two cornered rats, apparently forgotten. We held the entire firing line.

We slowly made our way towards our only exit at the foot of the cliff, gaining more courage with every step. Just to show the Turks that the British still had fight left in them, we fired an occasional bomb in their direction though I must admit I did not pay much attention to my aim. I was more concerned with making a noise and living long enough to reach the hole in the cliff.

Whether our defiant gesture had any influence on the sheltering troops I do not know but they returned to their vacated Line and we re-entered our gallery and commenced work as though nothing had interrupted us. I expected an officer or NCO to come down and explain why we had not been told of the intention to vacate the line but no one came and no explanation was ever given. I suppose a message had been sent to us but the messenger, more concerned with his own safety than ours, hopped out quickly whilst the going was good. I could understand his anxiety to live a little longer. After all, it was Christmas Day – a day to be born, not to die.

When our reliefs arrived and were told of the day's happenings, they were not as amused as we were now it was all over. Back at our shelter on Geogheghan's Bluff we sat around singing carols. So ended my first Christmas Day on active service; I had not even smelt a Christmas pudding!

Sunday, December 26th

The Turks bombarded the whole line from the Aegean to the Straits from dawn to late evening. They seem to have plenty of ammunition; this is the fourth day of systematic shelling, shrapnel and high explosives that leave a heavy pall of black smoke after their deafening crash. Our own artillery seems to have given the few shells they possessed to the Turks; only an occasional squib goes over to reply to the hundreds of Turkish coal boxes.

Upon entering the support line on our way to the gallery tonight we were instructed in a subdued whisper to wrap our feet with sandbags and not make the slightest sound, with no talking and no smoking. I could not understand what was going on. It was going to be very awkward to dig without making any noise. I cogitated on this on my way through the tunnel to the firing line in the Gully. I had not noticed anyone asleep, so why all this hush-hush nonsense?

When we reached the gallery we were told that as from yesterday there was to be a 'silence period' each night, the time and duration of these periods being altered nightly. At these times everyone in the firing line would have his feet swathed in sandbags to muffle his footfalls; all equipment that might jangle had to be discarded; there was to be no talking or smoking; no Verey Lights were to be fired and there was to be no rifle fire. The Turkish patrols were to be ignored unless they came within our wire.

These spells of silence were uncanny and yet we were allowed to continue digging. I had the feeling the whole world was listening to the noise of my digging. We are almost directly underneath the Turkish redoubt and they cannot help hearing us, which seems to make utter nonsense of the whole idea. Tonight's period was of two hours' duration. Even the working party carried out the filled sandbags in silence. The air was much cleaner as the no-talking ban also included swearing. There is nothing like a good swear word to make things go the way you want them and the work suffered accordingly. Trying to be a choir-boy when you are a trooper is very difficult, to say the least. When the silence period was over the working party gave vent to their feelings with added stress when they bumped their heads in the dark, as they often did. The air returned to normal.

Tuesday, December 28th

We have reached our final position underneath the Turkish redoubt and are busy making two recesses for the two charges in readiness for the 'Day'. We have been told that the mines will be larger than usual as the redoubt above us must be blown out of existence so that our troops can join up with those on the other side of the Gully. Extra tamping would be needed to counteract the added blast.

Wednesday, December 29th

Everything was ready and the troops were assembled. At the appointed moment the plunger was pushed down and the re-doubt that had held up our advance across the Gully on the nineteenth ceased to exist.

In a matter of minutes the Royal Scots Fusiliers were firmly established across the Gully. A communication trench that ran from the redoubt to the Turkish main line was barricaded and used as an advanced bombing sap. Between forty and fifty prisoners were taken. The usual firing went on all day and most of the night but our men held on to their gains.

Thursday, December 30th

Early in the morning the Turks began shelling our new positions across the Gully and kept it up for the rest of the day.

Attacking in the evening, they recaptured the bombing post but their occupation of this strategic point was cut short by a counter-attack.

These local attacks are minor incidents in the general plan yet some of the fiercest hand-to-hand fighting of the whole campaign takes place during them. Only those who have taken part in such attacks have any idea of the terrific strain they entail.

During the night the lads who had made the attack were relieved by men of a new division. They are strangers to me and must have landed recently.

Friday, December 31st

The usual bombardment all day; it seemed, to be concentrated on the Gully. The Turks attacked and again recaptured the bombing post. Again they were thrown out, this time by the new troops who do not appear to be new at fighting. It is getting quite a habit – sharing this miserable ten yards stretch of communication trench that was once the Turk's connecting link with their redoubt. I suppose they want it back because they dug it. For my part, they can have it and the foot of mud in the bottom. We have enough mud in our own lines; if this bitterly cold rain does not ease up we shall soon be unable to move. If you stand for a while, your feet are held so fast in the filthy stuff that it is as much as you can do to get loose. Some of the trenches have two feet of water in them whilst in others the water has seeped away, leaving two feet of mud. It is also very cold.

CHAPTER FOURTEEN

JANUARY, 1916

Saturday, January 1st, 1916

The beginning of the New Year. It looks much the same as the old one and shells instead of bells heralded it in.

With others of my team, I spent the whole day and much of the night carrying Ammonal from a dump in the Gully to the firing line. We finally cleared the dump and then slept there.

Sunday, January 2nd

The dump was fully replenished overnight I didn't hear a sound – it must have floated in on the wind – but where did it come from? There is a strange silence today. Yesterday we concentrated our efforts solely on the left of the Gully and we only occasionally met anyone. Today we are operating on the right of the Gully in the Eastern Birdcage sector. There do not appear to be any troops between the support lines and the beaches. I walked about for hours and did not meet anyone other than in the firing line.

I had a queer feeling of relief when, during the afternoon, our party was ordered to prepare the galleries for blasting. As we filled the sandbags for tamping I felt less alone. I had the company of live men and felt better with someone to talk to.

In two of the galleries some of our men were working as usual. They had the surprise of their lives when we brought down a hundred pounds of Ammonal as normally the explosive is not brought down until all work has been finished – but nothing seems to be normal any more.

Monday, January 3rd

Today we were told that Anzac and Suvla Bay had been evacuated but we were to hold on to Cape Helles. The news of the evacuation stunned us. Had we really admitted defeat? Had all the suffering been wasted and what of the dead?

During the morning we were ordered to stop digging in our particular gallery. We could quite easily hear the Turks mining. It was thought that if we continued to go forward there was a risk that we would get too close too soon. We would therefore make the Turks believe that we were digging as usual by banging our shovels on the floor of the gallery. We made the mine ready to blast at a few minutes' notice and our reliefs carried on as we had, banging their shovels.

At about noon we were rigging up waterproof sheets in the support trench to make it look as though it was occupied when an enemy plane flew over very low. I saw the pilot quite plainly. We greeted him with rapid fire but he continued on his way quite unconcernedly and to no great hurry.

With this excitement over we carried on with our job of make-believe. As we moved along the trench we came upon a small dug-out which appeared to have been some sort of headquarters. I observed an official notice pinned to a board which read: 'The VIIIth Army Corps will be relieved by the IXth AC. Inform all concerned.' I did not learn till afterwards that this was a piece of camouflage meaning that we would be evacuated about January 9th.

Until reading this notice I had been wondering if the authorities had forgotten that the VIIIth Army Corps existed – in fact I wondered if it had already gone. The French had gone, I knew, as the Royal Naval Division had vacated their brand new 'rest camp' on the high ground above 'X' Beach and taken over the French sector on the extreme right of the line.

I have no regrets about the absence of the French; I think we shall be much better off now they have gone.

I have lost sight of the 42nd Division; they, too, must have been relieved. Maybe we will be next. The Royal Naval Division is the only Division that has been here throughout the whole campaign. What was left of my battalion, the Hood, did have a few days on the Island of Imbros, a couple of hours' sail away, after the debacle of June 4th. (I was left behind to look after the stores.)

The 29th Division, with whom we landed, were withdrawn to take part in the Suvla landing in August but they are now with us at Cape Helles. The 52nd Division did not arrive, until July. The 'new' division is the 13th. I have not heard of them before. They are one of the divisions who landed at Suvla Bay and Anzac for the operations in that area and have been there ever since. A few days ago they took over the extreme left from the 29th Division. They belong to the IXth Army Corps so there is some truth in the notice I read.

What I cannot understand is why we are making believe the support trenches are occupied. If they are to be, why make believe? Why are we placing tons of explosive in galleries that are not ready; if it were to explode now it would not do much damage to the Turkish lines but would certainly make a mess of our own. No, we are not the only ones making believe – somebody is pulling our legs. In the meantime we have to get on with our bluffing like little schoolboys.

Tuesday, January 4th

During the last few days our little world has changed. It has split into two – activity in the firing line and on the beaches. In between there is emptiness – a labyrinth inhabited by ghosts. You do not see them; you only feel them. They follow you about all the time. The masses of barbed wire that prevent passage down this or that trench, the twelve-feet thick mass that stretches across the whole Peninsula in front of the Eski Line, the coils outside the communication trenches at selected spots out of sight of the enemy, do not impede the phantoms. Direction does not fool them. They have no sense of time, daylight or darkness makes no difference. Their world seems so peaceful. They are tranquil, with no fear of the hours that lie ahead, no recrimination and no hatred.

Late in the afternoon I made my way to the Worcester Barricade by way of Frith Walk, Chelmsford Street and, finally, Rue de Paris. In normal circumstances it would have been quite simple. Today it was difficult as the trenches were blocked by wire. I retraced my steps so many times that for a while I was hopelessly lost in a sector I normally knew well.

I was not in the best of moods when, having arrived in the gallery, I was told that I must not do any digging but when the Turks stopped digging I must bang my shovel on the floor so that they could hear us. One minute we are trying to make them believe that we have gone home and the next making sure he knows we are still here. Yesterday, in the Eastern Birdcage sector, there was a perfectly good reason for not getting too close; the Turks were quite near and we would profit by waiting for them to come into our net. Today, when it would be to our advantage to get much nearer to him, we are stuck here almost in our own front Line in this particular gallery. I am sure this nonsense will drive me mad.

Many of the communicating trenches are blocked with barbed wire. Not a soul is to be seen in the support lines and our guns seldom fire. There is a vast emptiness between us in the firing line and the intense activity on the beaches. All the existing galleries are filled with the highest known explosives and we are hardly allowed to breathe during the 'silence periods' in case the Turks hear our sighs – yet here am I fooling about with a shovel to attract their attention.

The official notice said we were to be relieved by the IXth Army Corps. It did not say precisely to which Nation this Army Corps belongs. If it is British, we are making it very difficult for them to reach us. If it is Turkish they, too, will have to tread warily. Given time, we will give them a hot reception – the earth will rise to meet them.

My daydream was broken by the arrival of our reliefs. I passed on the instructions that had been given me; they merely smiled. They had been down for the rations, etc., but again there was no mail. It is over two weeks now since we had any – I wonder why? Maybe some bright intelligence officer is afraid we might learn of the sudden evacuation of Anzac and Suvla Bay. This curtailment of our mail is most unwise as it lowers our morale by making our isolation complete. It is bad enough to be out of touch with the rest of our Army but it is tragic to be out of touch with the whole world. We feel forgotten and deserted.

Back to Geoghegan's Bluff, we were only just in time to say 'Good-bye' to a dozen of our sapper friends. They said they were on their way to England and promised to write to us upon ' reaching home.

'In the meantime,' they said, 'don't let the Turks catch you, They do all sorts of funny things to their prisoners before finally cutting their throats.'

They promised to tell the IXth Army Corps what good lads we had been and then maybe they would let us have a few days' leave on one of the nastier islands – provided we had still escaped capture. The IXth Army Corps has become a huge joke. No one now seriously believes we will be relieved but I still cling to the hope.

Wednesday, January 5th

We have been taking explosives to the galleries and laying mines in the Vineyard Sector. So many more trenches, are blocked that we needed the aid of a guide. We are gradually moving across the Peninsula. We began on the extreme left and are now in the centre. It is a long walk from our base on the Bluff and we do not meet anyone on our travels behind the line. Unconsciously, we tread lightly in case our footsteps break the silence of this one huge graveyard. We are afraid we might awaken the dead. They cannot be comfortable and must have a feeling that they, too, are going to be deserted. I am ashamed of leaving so many of my pals behind. We all came here together, full of hope and in the furtherance of that hope many have died. Their hopes and their bones are scattered in this desolate waste we are about to desert. We may escape with our bodies, but our souls will forever be with those who are beyond bodily escape. Those of us who survive will be tormented by this fiasco even though it was no fault of ours. We fought well and suffered dreadfully. We could not do more but in the end we deserted them.

It is so peaceful at the moment with no shelling or rifle-fire to disturb my thoughts.

Thursday, January 6th

We were in the line on the extreme left before six o'clock in the morning. We brought up more explosives and were busy laying mines until noon. We were then called upon to assist in repairing the firing line as several direct hits had damaged the parapet during the preceding half-hour. The barbed wire thrown into the trench was thrown back and additional sand-bags added where needed, making this particular spot stronger than it had ever been.

Everyone was very busy like Diogenes with his tub; some digging, some carrying explosives and others coils of barbed wire. The whole line was seething with life and the look-outs seemed keener than ever. The atmosphere was exceedingly tense and conversation was limited.

We left our base to collect another load of fireworks. We were about to begin our return journey when we were told quite casually that we would be evacuating the Peninsula. Today is 'X' day and 'Y' and 'Z' days will be determined by the progress made. We had, of course, known this for some time, yet this official notification, so casually given, stupefied me. I was extremely angry as I had for a long time cherished the hope that some day I would leave this inhospitable graveyard, defiant and with my head held high. I could not admit, even to myself, that we had been beaten after the sacrifice of so many men. Many are lying where they fell. Only a few graves have any visible indication that a few inches beneath the sand lies the remains of a human being; thousands have no known grave.

If the Turks attacked and drove us into the sea, then and only then would I admit defeat. The Turks are good fighters and to be beaten by such foes would not be a disgrace but to desert our fallen comrades and sneak away in the dark without a fight is a revolting thing and the thought of it nauseates me.

Throughout the whole campaign we have been starved of food, men and materials; in some quarters we have even been starved of good wishes. To those people who have been playing ducks and drakes with human life there will come a day of reckoning – they have a lot to answer for. In spite of starvation we have beaten the Turks on many occasions and, given a handful more men, could have overrun Achi Baba and dominated the Peninsula.

Friday, January 7th

We were again on the extreme left flank via Burnley Road, Come Street, Forward Inch, the Western Birdcage and Fifth Avenue. Every gallery had to have its quota of explosive and most of them were ready for firing.

At about eleven in the morning the Turks began an intensive bombardment of both sides of the Gully Ravine. It was soon obvious that this was the prelude to an attack. The question was – 'How long did we have to wait?' As the hours passed, thousands of shells crashed into the empty support trenches and those that fell in the front line took their toll. It was by far the most severe and prolonged shelling I have ever experienced. At about 3 pm. it was further intensified and at 3.30 pm. there was a terrific crash followed by yet another upheaval – two mines had gone up. Now came the attack! The Turks charged over, shouting wildly. They had about a hundred yards to cover before reaching my particular part of the line though they had less ground to cover a little further to the left.

After their four and a half hours' warning, we were ready for them. There was no doubt in our minds that it was their intention to drive us over the cliffs. Now that Anzac and Suvla Bay had been evacuated we were outnumbered by at least five to one. They came in their hundreds, some carrying timber for use to bridging our trenches. Perhaps they thought that after these hours of shelling there would be no one to stop them, but they had not reckoned with the Staffordshires of the 13th Division and eight sappers who could handle rifles as well as the rest. We should be able to – we have had plenty of practice. We blazed away at the advancing Turks who did not now appear to be in such a hurry to get to the coast. Some were becoming hesitant when our warships helped them to make up their minds. I thought the Navy had deserted us long ago and it was very heartening to hear their salvos. We certainly needed their help. Our resident squibs are few and far between nowadays but no doubt they do their little best and a good little best at that.

As the sun went down behind us and into the eyes of the Turks the attack petered out. I do not know the exact time as my faithful watch had been knocked about a bit but it was roughly 6 pm.

The battle was over and the drive to the sea had ended where it started. Intermittent shell and rifle fire persisted but though there was considerable activity near the Turkish lines throughout the night, no further attempt was made on our positions. They were no doubt collecting their dead and wounded; they must have suffered enormous losses. So long as they restricted their movements in the region of their wire we did not disturb them. We had beaten them but we knew they had plenty of reserves now that we had given up our other bridgeheads. They would come again with fresh troops.

We did not expect any rest, nor did we get much. Throughout the night we were alternately on look-out on the firestep for one hour and sleeping the next and so on. Everyone was too keyed up to sleep though. We did not want to be caught napping at this late hour. My watch has suffered irrepairable damage by the look of it.

Saturday, January 8th

After a cool night the dawn reminded me of long-gone spring dawns when I loved to roam among the heather. The air was so refreshing as the sun rose over the hills, causing the mist in the valleys to float away. The serenity enchanted me. The war seemed far away and hatred and strife non-existent – a world of peace. I was glad to be alive and wanted to stay alive yet I knew this would be difficult. Yesterday was terrible; what would today bring?

We think that today is 'Z' day, the day of our intended departure, but this depends on many things, Firstly the guns must go, then the horses, then the mules. After these the supporting troops must all have left before the line is given up. Only a specified number can be evacuated during the hours of darkness. The trawlers and lighters must make many journeys full to capacity, and must leave at the appointed time to enable them to return for more. If the men are to get away the sea must be reasonably calm. More than a slight swell would tear away our pontoons and our chances would go with them.

Now we have only the remnants of four divisions, about 16,000 weary men, half of them in the firing line. We do not know who is to remain to the end. Maybe on the beaches there is competition as to who shall be last to leave but we have over three miles to walk after we leave the line, two and a half hours' journey provided there is no interruption. We must wait and take our turn.

To those who have already left and those about to leave we say 'Good Luck'. We know we cannot all leave at the same time as there are not enough boats. The beaches are always shelled at night and, if the Turks become aware that we are leaving, every gun – and they have plenty – will be trained on the embarkation piers and barges alongside.

We have been told that the withdrawal from Anzac and Suvla Bay was carried out without the loss of a single man. Maybe we, too, will slip away unnoticed in the darkness though the element of surprise must have gone. Perhaps the Turks are thankful we are leaving but it would be a great boost to their morale if they were able to throw us out with great loss instead of having to admit they had been fooled for the second time within a month.

These are my own thoughts. We did not discuss evacuation at this late hour but we know in our own hearts that the odds are against us all getting away. After the beating we gave the Turks yesterday they may have second thoughts about our leaving at the moment. In the firing Line we have only one thought – self-preservation. Each of us firmly believes he has the right to live but we will not shirk our responsibilities.

Dusk was upon us and we eight sappers were ordered to unload our rifles. I took a parting shot at the enemy.

With the breech of my rifle empty but the magazine full, I returned with the others to our base at Geoghegan's Bluff to await further orders. We were given one day's rations and, as the waning moon set, started on our way across the Peninsula, our feet swathed in sandbags to muffle our footfalls.

About an hour's walk through the lonely and deserted support lines brought us to the Krithia Road, so well known to us. It was difficult to define exactly where we were but I think we had come along the trench which we knew as Wigan Road and halted where it cut across 'B' Avenue. Here we were issued with a piece of bandage which had to be worn on the arm to facilitate counting at the control posts on the way down.

We joined the tail end of a party from the line and went on our way to the beach. As we slowly tramped through the mud, a foot deep in many places, weary and very tired, I could not believe we were leaving. I expected every moment to be told to 'About-turn'.

It was a long while since I had closed my eyes for more than a few brief seconds but the thought of a remote chance of living kept me awake. Each painful step was a foot nearer to freedom, but there were many steps to three miles. As we halted at the control posts I instantly fell asleep, instinct waking me when the party moved off. We were all the same – walking aimlessly and in a stupor.

A cool breeze brought my slumbers to an end. We were in the open a long way from the firing line and approaching 'V' beach. It was very dark as the moon had set. It was strangely quiet; no one had time for words. We were all living in the past. The future did not exist any more – it was so very far away and the past so near, so fresh in our minds. I imagined all my pals were with me as they had been on the day we landed. We had been a motley crowd, full of hope then and anxious to do our best for Britain. Our Colonel had told us the eyes of the world would be upon us. The eyes of the Turks certainly were but the rest of the world forgot us. Maybe in years to come they will remember but it will be too late.

The battle is over and the time has come for us to take our leave. The sole survivor of my section, I went on my weary way towards the sea, leaving the bodies of my pals to enrich the Turkish soil; I hope they will understand.

The pace quickened a little as we were behind schedule. As we climbed the slight slope leading to the cliffs, we heard the bugler at the fort on Sedd el Bahr sound a long 'G'. He had observed the flash of the firing of Asiatic Annie. We had a little less than half a minute to take cover but as we were on open ground there was nowhere to shelter. We plodded forward towards where we knew the shell was probably aimed. With a resounding thud it fell directly ahead of us over the brow of the hill. If the shelling was of the usual type we should have reached the shelter of the cliffs before the next shell arrived.

When we reached the cliffs we sat awaiting our turn to leave. The bugler again sounded his warning note and more weary men came to the cliffs for shelter. The shell fell close to the rickety pier and hurrying figures disappeared in the darkness. There was another warning note and another crash; more hurrying figures and more waiting.

It was past midnight when my party was ordered to make for the pier and to board an iron lighter under the shadow of the River Clyde. There was a heavy swell running and we went below with difficulty. It was so crammed with men that it was impossible to raise one's hand to stifle a sneeze. The stench was overpowering. Some men were sick, some fainted but could not fall and many were fast asleep – in spite of the occasion. No others came aboard and there was not room for even one more but we still waited.

Asiatic Annie, the gun we had laughed at hundreds of times, was now less of a joke. She was a menace and was threatening our escape. Imprisoned in this iron tomb we were helpless, so near to escape and yet so near to death.

The lighter rolled as another shell struck the water. The rolling increased and a mass of exhausted humanity left the shore they could not see; a load of garbage to be dumped somewhere and forgotten. Perhaps as the years roll by we will be remembered as the expedition that was betrayed by jealousy, spite, indecision and treachery.

The Turks did not beat us – we were beaten by our own High Command!